Social Issues
in Literature

Racism in
The Autobiography of Malcolm X

Other Books in the Social Issues in Literature Series:

Social Issues
in Literature

Racism in
The Autobiography of
Malcolm X

Candice Mancini, Book Editor

GREENHAVEN PRESS
A part of Gale, Cengage Learning

Detroit • New York • San Francisco • New Haven, Conn • Waterville, Maine • London

GALE
CENGAGE Learning™

Christine Nasso, *Publisher*
Elizabeth Des Chenes, *Managing Editor*

© 2009 Greenhaven Press, a part of Gale, Cengage Learning

Gale and Greenhaven Press are registered trademarks used herein under license.

For more information, contact:
Greenhaven Press
27500 Drake Rd.
Farmington Hills, MI 48331-3535
Or you can visit our Internet site at gale.cengage.com

For product information and technology assistance, contact us at

Gale Customer Support, 1-800-877-4253
For permission to use material from this text or product, submit all requests online at www.cengage.com/permissions

Further permissions questions can be emailed to permissionrequest@cengage.com

Articles in Greenhaven Press anthologies are often edited for length to meet page requirements. In addition, original titles of these works are changed to clearly present the main thesis and to explicitly indicate the author's opinion. Every effort is made to ensure that Greenhaven Press accurately reflects the original intent of the authors. Every effort has been made to trace the owners of copyrighted material.

Cover photograph reproduced by permission of Burt Shavitz/Pix Inc./Time Life Pictures/Getty Images.

LIBRARY OF CONGRESS CATALOGING-IN-PUBLICATION DATA

Racism in The autobiography of Malcolm X / Candice Mancini, book editor.
   p. cm. -- (Social issues in literature)
   Includes bibliographical references and index.
   ISBN-13: 978-0-7377-4260-2 (hbk.)
   ISBN-13: 978-0-7377-4261-9 (pbk.)
   1. X, Malcolm, 1925-1965. Autobiography of Malcolm X. 2. African American Muslims--Biography. 3. Racism in literature. 4. Racism--United States. 5.African American authors--Biography--History and criticism. I. Mancini, Candice.
   BP223.Z8.L5767 2008
   320.54'6092--dc22

                                                          2008021485

Contents

Chapter 2: *The Autobiography of Malcolm X* and Racism

Introduction

The *Autobiography of Malcolm X* is more than the story of a black man living in a landscape of racism. *The Autobiography* makes apparent the complexity of this landscape. It demonstrates why there are no easy solutions when it comes to race relations in America and why now, 40 years after the passing of civil rights for African Americans, the relationship between black and white remains strained. It helps to explain why 140 years after slavery was abolished, blacks continue to experience higher rates of crime, poverty, disease, and unemployment than whites. During his years as a Nation of Islam leader, Malcolm X vehemently opposed white involvement in the civil rights movement, urging blacks to separate themselves from whites, whom he often referred to as "devils." For this, Malcolm himself has often been labeled a racist. But the story is not so simple.

The racism Malcolm X, born Malcolm Little, faced in his life varied from barefaced and violent to deceiving and hypocritical. When Malcolm's mother was pregnant with him, the Ku Klux Klan (KKK) threatened the Little household with guns; when he was four years old, white supremacists burned their house to the ground. Malcolm's father, who had lost three brothers at the hands of white men, died under violent yet mysterious circumstances and was thought to have been killed by white supremacists. The less obvious effects of racism were also damaging, as when a "kindly" schoolteacher told Malcolm he could not realistically become a lawyer because he was a "n[-----]."

Even when looking through the singular lens of Malcolm's experience, it seems logical that he would be distrustful of whites. But as Malcolm learned during his period of self-education in prison—a time when, he said, "you couldn't have gotten me out of books with a wedge,"—American racism was a disease that began with slavery and thrived on hate. It was a condition built on a relationship between oppressor and oppressed, abuser and abused, enslaver and enslaved. Even after slavery was abolished, the situation for blacks remained bleak; the system of abuse and violence continued, perpetrated by many and sanctioned by the law. As black historian Roger Wilkins put it in a 1995 article for *The Nation*: "blacks have a 375-year history on this continent: 245 involving slavery, 100 involving legal discrimination, and only 30 involving anything else."

The legal discrimination to which Wilkins refers involved laws nearly as ruthless as slavery and held sway from the ratification of the 13th Amendment in 1865 through to the passage of the Civil Rights Act in 1964. Southern Black Codes, enacted after slaves were freed, were meant to keep blacks "in their place," meaning as close to slavery as possible. Codes made it illegal for blacks to be unemployed, be in debt, to vote, and to have sex with white women. Most blacks, youths and adults, had curfews. The Jim Crow laws that followed banned blacks from public places, including restaurants, hospitals, parks, and schools. The 1896 Supreme Court case of *Plessy v. Ferguson* legalized discrimination by establishing that it was not unconstitutional for facilities between blacks and whites to be "separate but equal." As for "equal," there were little, if any, efforts to make facilities for blacks equal to those for whites. It was not until the 1954 Supreme Court case of *Brown v. Board of Education* that legal segregation was overturned.

The 1964 Civil Rights Act was the first legislation that made racial discrimination illegal. That same year, Malcolm announced he was open to working with whites in his movement. But the two were not connected: it was Malcolm's recent trip to Mecca and his break from Nation of Islam leader Elijah Muhammad, not the 1964 Civil Rights Act, that altered his ideas. While Malcolm remained distrustful of American whites, his experience with interracial brotherhood in Mecca revealed to him possibilities larger than America. As Malcolm put it, in Mecca they were "white, black, brown, red, yellow people, blue eyes and blond hair, and my kinky red hair—all together, brothers!" Regrettably, Malcolm was killed within a year, leaving unanswered the question of how much hope he would have held for white/black brotherhood in America.

There is, however, no question about the volatile reactions to the 1964 Civil Rights Act. Later that year, three civil rights activists working to register black voters in Mississippi were murdered by the KKK, their bodies later found in a dam. In Selma, Alabama, peaceful civil rights marchers on their way to Montgomery were hospitalized after police attacked them with whips, clubs, and tear gas. Race riots broke out in a black section of Los Angeles called Watts.

It is not that 1964 was unique in its episodes of violence toward blacks, but it was a reminder that one piece of legislation was merely a start. Even now, there remain racial problems for which there are no simple answers. As Roger Wilkins said on the television show *A NewsHour with Jim Lehrer* in 2000, "The problem of race in this country is so deep and so close to the center of American culture and so close to the psyches of so many people that it's going to take massive undertakings by a range of American institutions to wipe out what remains, and what remains is a pretty killing for lots of human beings."

The following articles investigate racism as illustrated in Malcolm X's *Autobiography* and explore how race relations in the U.S. remain complex.

Chronology

1919

Malcolm X's parents, Earl Little (a Baptist minister and follower of Marcus Garvey's black nationalism) and Louise Norton, are married.

1925

Malcolm X is born on May 19, in Omaha, Nebraska, to Earl and Louise Little. He is the fourth of their seven children.

1926

The Little family moves to Milwaukee, Wisconsin.

1928

The Littles move to Lansing, Michigan.

1929

The Littles' house in Lansing is set on fire and burns down. Later, Malcolm attributes the act to white supremacists. Earl Little builds a new house in East Lansing.

1931

Earl Little is killed in a streetcar accident, leaving the Little family in financial distress. Malcolm later states that white supremacists are to blame for the death.

1939

Louise Little is declared mentally ill and sent to the Kalamazoo State Mental Hospital, where she will remain for 26 years. Malcolm's siblings are placed with various foster families while Malcolm is sent to a juvenile home in the nearly all-white community of Mason, Michigan.

1940

At 15 years of age, Malcolm visits his half-sister Ella Collins in Boston. The trip proves to be a life-changing experience.

1941

Ella Collins gains custody of Malcolm, and he moves to Boston with her. Malcolm becomes a zoot-suit-wearing "hipster" and gains the nickname "Detroit Red." He begins dating Sophia, a white woman. In Boston he finds various jobs, including one working for the railroad. The railroad takes Malcolm to New York for the first time, and he moves there soon after.

1944

Malcolm is indicted for larceny and receives a three-month suspended sentence and one year of probation.

1945

Malcolm moves back to Boston, where he becomes heavily involved in robberies with his friend Malcolm Jarvis and three white women. One of the women is his girlfriend, Sophia.

1946

Malcolm and the others are arrested for grand larceny, breaking and entering, and firearms possession. Malcolm and Jarvis receive a sentence of eight to ten years, while Sophia serves seven months. The court tries to convince the white women to charge Malcolm and Jarvis of rape, but they refuse. Malcolm remains imprisoned until 1952.

1947

In jail Malcolm meets a man he calls "Bimbi," who encourages Malcolm to read and study.

1948

Malcolm is convinced by his family members to study the words of Elijah Muhammad, leader of the Nation of Islam.

1952

Malcolm is released on parole and moves in with his brother, Wilfred, in Detroit. He joins the Nation of Islam and changes his surname from "Little" to "X," claiming that the former is a slave name given by white racists. Malcolm begins recruiting for the Nation of Islam's Detroit temple, and within a year membership triples.

1953

Malcolm is appointed assistant minister of the Detroit temple. Later that year Elijah Muhammad sends him back to Boston to become Temple No. 11's first minister.

1954

Malcolm becomes chief minister of Harlem's Temple No. 7.

1957

After New York Temple member Johnson Hinton is beaten by police, Malcolm goes to the Harlem precinct headquarters, demanding that Hinton receive medical care. Hinton is then brought to a nearby hospital, where a Muslim crowd gathers. Police try to disperse the crowd, but the crowd does not leave until Malcolm raises his hand and waves. Malcolm sues New York City for police brutality, winning the largest settlement in its history.

1958

At the age of 32, Malcolm marries fellow Temple member Betty Sanders, who is 23 years old. Later that year their first child, Attallah, is born.

1959

Malcolm visits Ghana, Sudan, Nigeria, Iran, Syria, Egypt, and the United Arab Republic. Although he planned to travel to Mecca, he does not make it there.

1961

Malcolm is promoted to national representative of the Nation of Islam; other Temple members grow increasingly resentful of him.

1962

Malcolm discovers that his role model and father figure, Elijah Muhammad, has engaged in numerous instances of adultery and has fathered children with at least three of his secretaries.

1963

Malcolm begins work on his *Autobiography* with Alex Haley. Later that year, Malcolm makes his infamous "chickens coming home to roost" statement in response to the assassination of President John F. Kennedy. In reaction to the statement, Elijah Muhammad silences Malcolm for 90 days. The relationship between Muhammad and Malcolm has already been disintegrating because of Malcolm's spoken disapproval of Muhammad's adulterous affairs.

1964

Elijah Muhammad removes Malcolm as the Nation's national representative and minister of Harlem's Temple No. 7. Malcolm is later suspended "indefinitely" by the Nation of Islam. He announces plans to begin his own organization, "Muslim Mosque Incorporated," and predicts his assassination by Black Muslim leaders. He makes a pilgrimage to Mecca, where he is surprised to see black and white Muslims united in brotherhood.

1965

On February 14 Malcolm's family's home is firebombed. Malcolm states that the act was ordered by Elijah Muhammad. Seven days later, Malcolm X is assassinated while making a speech at an Organization of Afro-American Unity (OAAU) rally in Harlem. Three Nation of Islam members are later convicted of the assassination.

Social Issues
in Literature

CHAPTER 1

Background on Malcolm X and Alex Haley

The Life of Malcolm X

DISCovering Multicultural America

Malcolm X, born Malcolm Little in 1925, became one of the most controversial black leaders in history. Like most African-Americans of his time, Malcolm grew up under the restraints of racism. After spending much of his youth trying to fit in with white culture, Malcolm became an outspoken leader in the Nation of Islam, under Elijah Muhammad. At the core of Malcolm's preaching were black pride and distrust of whites. In his speeches he often took an especially unbending stance, calling all white people "devils." In 1964 he broke from Muhammad and became more tolerant of whites who shared a desire for racial justice. But the next year Malcolm was assassinated by members of the Nation of Islam. To this day, his message continues.

Malcolm X was one of the most fiery and controversial blacks of the twentieth century.

Born Malcolm Little in Omaha, Nebraska on May 19, 1925, Malcolm was the son of a Baptist minister, who was an avid supporter of Marcus Garvey's Universal Negro Improvement Association. While living in Omaha, the family was often harassed—at one point the family's house was set afire. In 1929 the family moved to Lansing, Michigan. While in Michigan, Malcolm's father was killed; his body severed in two by a streetcar and his head smashed. In his autobiography, written with Alex Haley, Malcolm asserted that his father may have been killed by members of the Ku Klux Klan. His mother, stricken by the death of her husband and the demands of providing for the family, was committed to a mental institution.

Leaving school after the eighth grade, Malcolm made his way to New York, working for a time as a waiter at Smalls

DISCovering Multicultural America, "Malcolm X: Biographical Essay," Online ed., 2003. Reproduced by permission of Gale, a part of Cengage Learning.

Paradise in Harlem. Malcolm began selling and using drugs, turned to burglary, and, in 1946, was sentenced to a ten-year prison term on burglary charges.

While in prison Malcolm became acquainted with the Black Muslim sect, headed by Elijah Muhammad, and was quickly converted. Following his parole in 1952, he soon became an outspoken defender of Muslim doctrines, accepting the basic argument that evil was an inherent characteristic of the "white man's Christian world."

Unlike Muhammad, Malcolm sought publicity, making provocative and inflammatory statements to predominantly white civic groups and college campus audiences. Branding white people "devils," he spoke bitterly of a philosophy of vengeance and "an eye for an eye." When, in 1963, he characterized the Kennedy assassination as a case of "chickens coming home to roost," he was suspended from the Black Muslim movement by Elijah Muhammad.

Disillusioned with Elijah Muhammad's teachings, Malcolm formed his own organizations, the Organization of Afro-American Unity and the Muslim Mosque Inc. In 1964 he made a pilgrimage to Islam's holy city, Mecca, and adopted the name El-Hajj Malik El Shabazz. He also adopted views that were not popular with other black nationalists, including the idea that not all whites were evil and that blacks could make gains by working through established channels.

As a result of Malcolm's new views, he became the victim of death threats. On February 14, 1965, his home was fire-bombed; his wife and children escaped unharmed. A week later, on the 21st, Malcolm was shot and killed at the Audubon Ballroom in Harlem, while preparing to speak. Three of the men arrested were later identified as members of the Nation of Islam.

Malcolm X had a profound influence on both blacks and whites. Many blacks responded to a feeling that he was a man of the people, experienced in the ways of the street rather than the pulpit or the college campus, which traditionally had provided the preponderance of black leaders. Many young whites responded to Malcolm's blunt, colorful language and unwillingness to retreat in the face of hostility.

The memory and image of Malcolm X has changed as much after his death as his own philosophies changed during his life. At first thought to be a violent fanatic, he is now understood as an advocate of self-help, self-defense, and education; as a philosopher and pedagogue, he succeeded in integrating history, religion, and mythology to establish a framework for his ultimate belief in world brotherhood and in human justice. Faith, in his view, was a prelude to action; ideas were feckless without policy. At least three books published since his death effectively present his most enduring thoughts. In 1992, a monumental film by Spike Lee based on his autobiography renewed interest and understanding in the meaning of the life and death of Malcolm X.

The Complex Identity of Malcolm X

"When I talk about my father," said Attallah Shabazz to *Rolling Stone*, "I do my best to make Malcolm human. I don't want these kids to keep him on the pedestal, I don't want them to feel his goals are unattainable. I'll remind them that at their age he was doing time." The powerful messages of Malcolm X, his dramatic life, and his tragic assassination conspire to make him an unreachable hero. Events in the 1960s provided four hero-martyrs of this kind for Americans: John F. Kennedy, Robert F. Kennedy, Rev. Martin Luther King, Jr., and Malcolm X. These idealistic men believed in the possibilities for social change, the necessity of that change, and the truth of his vision of change.

Of the four, Malcolm came from the humblest roots, was the most radical, most outspoken, and angriest—"All Negroes are angry, and I am the angriest of all," he often would say. The powerful speaker gathered huge crowds around him when

Malcolm X, born Malcolm Little in 1925, grew to become one of the most controversial black leaders in history. AP Images.

he was associated with Elijah Muhammad's Lost-Found Nation of Islam movement, and afterwards with Malcolm X's own organization. Many Americans, white and black, were afraid of the violent side of Malcolm X's rhetoric; unlike Rev. Martin Luther King, Jr.'s doctrine of non-violent resistance, Malcolm X believed in self-defense.

But Malcolm X cannot be summed up in a few convenient phrases, because during his life he went through distinct changes in his philosophies and convictions. He had three names: Malcolm Little, Malcolm X, and El-Hajj Malik El-Shabazz. Each name has its own history and illuminates a different facet of the man who remains one of the most compelling Americans of the 20th century.

Father's Influence

Malcolm X's father was a Baptist minister and a member of the United Negro Improvement Association. Founded by Marcus Garvey, the group believed that there could be no peace for blacks in America, and that each black person should return to their African nation to lead a natural and serene life. In a parallel belief, Nation of Islam supporters in Malcolm X's time held that a section of the United States [should] secede and become a nation onto itself for disenfranchised blacks. It seems possible that Malcolm X was predisposed to the separatist ideas of the Nation of Islam partly because of this early exposure to Marcus Garvey.

Malcolm X described in his autobiography (written with Alex Haley) the harassment of his father, including terrifying visits from the Ku Klux Klan; one of Malcolm X's first memories is of his home in Omaha burning down. The family moved to Lansing, Michigan in 1929, and there Malcolm X's memories were of his father's rousing sermons and the beatings the minister gave his wife and children. Malcolm X believed his father to be a victim of brainwashing by white people, who infected blacks with self-hatred—therefore he would pass down a form of the abuse he received as a black man.

The minister was killed in 1931, his body almost severed in two by a streetcar and the side of his head smashed. In the autobiography, Malcolm X elaborated, saying that there were many rumors in Lansing that his father had been killed by the

Klan or its ilk because of his preachings, and that he had been laid on the streetcar tracks to make his death appear accidental. After his father was killed, the state welfare representatives began to frequent the house, and it seemed to Malcolm X that they were harassing his mother. Terribly stricken by her husband's death and buckling under the demands of raising many children, Louise Little became psychologically unstable and was institutionalized until 1963.

Crime and Other Self-Degradation

After his mother was committed, Malcolm X began what was to be one of the most publicized phases of his life. His brothers and sisters were separated, and while living with several foster families, Malcolm began to learn to steal. In his autobiography, he used his own young adulthood to illustrate larger ideas about the racist climate in the United States. In high school, Malcolm began to fight what would be a lifelong battle of personal ambition versus general racist preconception. An English teacher discouraged Malcolm X's desire to become a lawyer, telling him to be "realistic," and that he should think about working with his hands.

Lansing did not hold many opportunities of *any* kind for a young black man then, so without a particular plan, Malcolm X went to live with his half-sister, Ella, in Boston. Ella encouraged him to look around the city and get a feel for it before trying to land a job. Malcolm X looked, and almost immediately found trouble. He fell in with a group of gamblers and thieves, and began shining shoes at the Roseland State Ballroom. There he learned the trades that would eventually take him to jail—dealing in bootleg liquor and illegal drugs. Malcolm X characterized his life then as one completely lacking in self-respect. Although his methods grew more sophisticated over time, it was only a matter of four years or so before he was imprisoned in 1946, sentenced to ten years on burglary charges.

Many journalists would emphasize Malcolm X's "shady" past when describing the older man, his clean-cut lifestyle, and the aims of the Nation of Islam. In some cases, these references were an attempt to damage Malcolm X's credibility, but economically disadvantaged people have found his early years to be a point of commonality, and Malcolm X himself was proud of how far he had come. He spared no detail of his youth in his autobiography, and used his Nation of Islam (sometimes called Black Islam) ideas to interpret them. Dancing, drinking and even his hair style were represented by Malcolm X to be marks of shame and self-hatred.

Relaxed hair in particular was an anathema to Malcolm X for the rest of his life; he described his first "conk" in the autobiography this way: "This was my first really big step toward self-degredation: when I endured all of that pain [of the hair-straightening chemicals], literally burning my flesh to have it look like a white man's hair. I had joined that multitude of Negro men and women in America who are brainwashed into believing that the black people are 'inferior'—and white people 'superior'—that they will even violate and mutilate their God-created bodies to try to look 'pretty' by white standards. . . . It makes you wonder if the Negro has completely lost his sense of identity, lost touch with himself."

Emerging from Prison a Muslim Leader

It was while Malcolm X was in prison that he was introduced to the ideas of Elijah Muhammad and the Nation of Islam. Fundamentally, the group believes in the racial superiority of blacks, a belief supported by a complex genesis fable, which includes an envious, evil white scientist who put a curse on blacks. The faith became a focus for Malcolm X's fury about his treatment (and his family's) at the hands of whites, about the lack of opportunity he had as a young black man, and the psychological damage of systematic anti-black racism—that is, the damage of self-hatred.

Malcolm X read "everything he could get his hands on" in the prison library. He interpreted history books with the newly-learned tenets of Elijah Muhammad, and told of his realizations in a *Playboy* interview with Alex Haley. "I found out that the history-whitening process either had left out great things that black men had done, or the great black men had gotten whitened." He improved his penmanship by copying out a dictionary, and participated in debates in jail, preaching independently to the prisoners about the Nation of Islam's theories about "the white devil." The group also emphasizes scrupulous personal habits, including cleanliness and perfect grooming, and forbids smoking, drinking, and the eating of pork, as well as other traditional Muslim dietary restrictions.

When Malcolm X left prison in 1952, he went to work for Elijah Muhammad, and within a year was named assistant minister to Muslim Temple Number One in Detroit, Michigan. It was then that he took the surname "X" and dropped his "slave name" of Little—the X stands for the African tribe of his origin that he could never know. The Nation of Islam's leadership was so impressed by his tireless efforts and his firey speeches that they sent him to start a new temple in Boston, which he did, then repeated his success in Philadelphia by 1954.

Malcolm X's faith was inextricably linked to his worship of Elijah Muhammad. Everything Malcolm X accomplished (he said) was accomplished through Elijah Muhammad. In his autobiography, he recalled a speech which described his devotion: "I have sat at our Messenger's feet, hearing the truth from his own mouth, I have pledged on my knees to Allah to tell the white man about his crimes and the black man the true teachings of our Honorable Elijah Muhammad. I don't care if it costs my life." His devotion would be sorely tested, then destroyed within nine years.

"Chickens Coming Home to Roost"

During those nine years, Malcolm X was made a national minister—he became the voice of the Nation of Islam. He was a speechwriter, an inspired speaker, a pundit often quoted in the news, and he became a philosopher. Malcolm used the teachings of the Nation of Islam to inform blacks about the cultures that had been stripped from them and the self-hatred that whites had inspired, then he would point the way toward a better life. While Rev. Martin Luther King, Jr., was teaching blacks to fight racism with love, Malcolm X was telling blacks to understand their exploitation, to fight back when attacked, and to seize self-determination "by any means necessary." Malcolm spoke publicly of his lack of respect for King, who would, through a white man's religion, tell blacks to not fight back.

In his later years, though, Malcolm X thought that he and King perhaps did have the same goals and that a truce was possible. While Malcolm X was in the process of questioning the Nation of Islam's ideals, his beliefs were in a creative flux. He began to visualize a new Islamic group which "would embrace all faiths of black men, and it would carry into practice what the Nation of Islam had only preached." His new visions laid the groundwork for a break from the Black Muslims.

In 1963 a conflict between Malcolm X and Elijah Muhammad made headlines. When President John F. Kennedy was assassinated, Malcolm said that it was a case of "chickens coming home to roost." *Rolling Stone* reported that many people believed Malcolm X had declared the president deserving of his fate, when he really "meant the country's climate of hate had killed the president." Muhammad suspended Malcolm X for ninety days "so that Muslims everywhere can be disassociated from the blunder," according to the autobiography.

Muhammad had been the judge and jury for the Nation of Islam, and had sentenced many other Black Muslims to terms of silence, or excommunication, for adultery or other infractions of their religious code. Malcolm X discovered that Muhammad himself was guilty of adultery, and was appalled by his idol's hypocrisy. It widened the gulf between them. Other minsters were vying for the kind of power and attention that Malcolm X had, and some speculate that these men filled Elijah Muhammad's ears with ungenerous speculations about Malcolm X's ambitions. "I hadn't hustled in the streets for years for nothing. I knew when I was being set up," Malcolm X said of that difficult time. He believed that he would be indefinitely silenced and that a Nation of Islam member would be convinced to assassinate him. Before that would come to pass, Malcolm X underwent another period of transformation, during which he would take on his third name, El-Hajj Malik El-Shabazz.

All Brothers Under Allah

A "hajj" is a pilgrimage to the holy land of Mecca, Saudi Arabia, the birthplace of the Prophet Muhammad; "Malik" was similar to Malcolm, and "Shabazz," a family name. On March 8, 1964, Malcolm X had announced that he was leaving the Nation of Islam to form his own groups, Muslim Mosque, Inc., and the Organization of Afro-American Unity. In an effort to express his dedication to Islam, and thereby establish a more educated religious underpinning for his new organization, Malcolm X declared he would make a hajj. His travels were enlarged to include a tour of Middle Eastern and African countries, including Egypt, Lebanon, Nigeria, and Ghana.

These expeditions would expand Malcolm X in ways that would have seemed incredible to him earlier. He encountered fellow Muslims who were caucasian and embraced him as a brother, he was accepted into the traditional Islamic religion, and he was lauded as a fighter for the rights of American blacks. "Packed in the plane [to Jedda] were white, black, brown, red, and yellow people, blue eyes and blond hair, and my kinky red hair—all together, brothers! All honoring the same God Allah, all in turn giving equal honor to the other."

As a result of his experiences, Malcolm X gained a burgeoning understanding of a global unity and sympathy that stood behind America's blacks—less isolated and more reinforced, he revised his formerly separatist notions.

Still full of resolve, Malcolm X returned to the States with a new message. He felt that American blacks should go to the United Nations and demand their rights, not beg for them. When faced with a bevy of reporters upon his return, he told them, "The true Islam has shown me that a blanket indictment of all white people is as wrong as when whites make blanket indictments against blacks." His new international awareness was evident in statements such as: "The white man's racism toward the black man here in America has got him in such trouble all over that world, with other nonwhite peoples."

His Influence Continues

This new message, full of renewed vigor and an enlarged vision, plus the fact that the media was still listening to Malcolm X, was not well-received by the Nation of Islam. Malcolm X was aware that he was being followed by Black Muslims, and regularly received death threats. His home was firebombed on February 14, 1965—his wife and four daughters were unharmed, but the house was destroyed, and the family had not been insured against fire. It was believed that the attack came from the Nation of Islam. A week later, Malcolm X, his wife (pregnant with twin girls), and four daughters went to the Audubon Ballroom in Harlem, New York, where he would speak for the last time. A few minutes into his message, three men stood and fired sixteen shots into Malcolm X, who died before medical help could arrive. The three were arrested immediately, and were later identified as members of the Nation of Islam.

Malcolm X gave African-Americans something no one else ever had—a sense that the race has a right to feel anger and express the power of it, to challenge white domination, and to actively demand change. Politically sophisticated, Malcolm X told everyone who would listen about the tenacious and pervasive restraints that centuries of racism had imposed on American blacks. His intelligence and humility was such that he was not afraid to revise his ideas, and he held up the example of his transformations for all to see and learn from.

Although Malcolm X's own organizations were unsteady at the time of his death, the posthumous publication of his autobiography insures that his new and old philosophies will never be forgotten. Years after his assassination, Malcolm X and his ideas are still a huge component in the ongoing debate about race relations. Plays and movies focus on him, new biographies are written, and several colleges and societies survive him. "Malcolm's maxims on self-respect, self-reliance and economic empowerment seem acutely prescient," said *Newsweek* in 1990. The words of Malcolm X and the example of his life still urge Americans to fight racism in all of its forms.

The Life of Alex Haley

Marilyn Kern-Foxworth

Marilyn Kern-Foxworth is an associate professor of journalism at Texas A&M University and the author of Aunt Jemima, Uncle Ben, and Rastus: Blacks in Advertising, Yesterday, Today, and Tomorrow *(1994).*

Alex Haley began writing out of boredom while serving in the U.S. Coast Guard as a messboy on an ammunition ship. At age 37, retired from the Coast Guard and living in a basement apartment in New York City, Haley was barely scraping by as a freelance writer. But things improved and he began receiving paid magazine assignments. One of these assignments, an interview with Black Muslim leader Malcolm X, led to the 1965 publication of The Autobiography of Malcolm X. *The book became an immediate best-seller. Still, it was his 1976 book* Roots: The Saga of an American Family—*which traced his ancestors back to Gambia, West Africa—that turned his writing career into a phenomenal success.*

Alex Murray Palmer Haley was born 11 August 1921 in Ithaca, New York, and reared in the small town of Henning, Tennessee. He was the oldest of three sons born to Bertha George Palmer and Simon Alexander Haley. When he was born, both parents were in their first year of graduate school, Bertha at the Ithaca Conservatory of Music, and Simon at Cornell University. They took the young Alex to Henning, where he grew up under the influence of women who inspired his search for his past. He remembers listening for hours as his family reminisced about an African ancestor who refused to respond to the slave name "Toby." "They said anytime any

Marilyn Kern-Foxworth, *Dictionary of Literary Biography, Volume 38: Afro-American Writers After 1955, Dramatists and Prose Writers.* Detroit, MI: Gale, 1985. Reproduced by permission of Gale, a part of Cengage Learning.

of the other slaves called him that, he would strenuously re-buff them, declaring that his name was 'Kin-tay.'" These initial stories would serve as the basis for his 1976 novel *Roots: The Saga of an American Family*.

Not a stellar student in high school, Haley graduated with a C average at the age of fifteen. He then entered Alcorn A & M College in Lorman, Mississippi. After a short period, he transferred to Elizabeth City State Teachers College in North Carolina, from which he withdrew at age seventeen.

A Writing Life

His experiences after college contributed directly to his growth as a writer. In 1939 he enlisted in the U.S. Coast Guard as a messboy. To alleviate the boredom he experienced while cruis-ing in the southwestern Pacific aboard an ammunition ship, he began writing. His first venture included writing love let-ters for his shipmates. He expanded his range with articles that he submitted to several American magazines. A series of rejection slips followed before his first article was accepted for publication by *This Week*, a syndicated Sunday newspaper supplement.

When Haley retired from the coast guard at the age of thirty-seven, he had attained the position of chief journalist. Although he had dutifully served twenty years in the coast guard, he was not permitted to collect his pension checks—those were given as child support to Nannie Branch, whom he had married in 1941. They had two children, William Alex-ander and Lydia Ann. They were separated for several years before getting divorced in 1964, the year he married Juliette Collins, whom he subsequently divorced; they had one child, Cynthia Gertrude.

Determined to continue his avid interest in writing, Haley moved into a basement apartment in New York City's Green-wich Village where, as a freelance writer, he lived a penurious existence. He was in debt and saw no brightness in his immediate future: "I owed everyone. One day a friend called with a Civil Service job that paid $6000 per year. I turned it down. I wanted to make it writing. My friend banged the phone down. I owed him too. I took psychic inventory. I looked in the cupboard, and there were two cans of sardines, marked two for 21 cents. I had 18 cents in a sack and I said to myself that I'd keep them." As a reminder of what he had to endure to get to where he is today, Haley framed the coins and cans and displays them in his private library; he calls them a symbol of his "determination to be independent," and vows that they will always be on the wall.

Haley's life soon took a turn for the better. The day after taking inventory of his circumstances, Haley received a check for an article he had written. This small reward fell short of the recognition he desired, but it did presage the beginning of assignments from more and more magazines, one of which was *Reader's Digest*, where he later published the first excerpts from *Roots*.

Success with Malcolm X

Eventually, Haley's commitment to writing paid off in two significant ways. First, he received an assignment from *Playboy* in 1962 to interview jazz trumpeter Miles Davis, which led to the establishment of the "Playboy Interview," a new series for the magazine. Second, he was asked to write a feature about Black Muslim leader Malcolm X. This interview was the impetus for Haley's writing the best-selling *The Autobiography of Malcolm X* (1965), which sold 50,000 hardcover copies and about five million copies in paperback.

The Autobiography of Malcolm X traces Malcolm Little's transformation into Malcolm X, signifying his belief that black people in America had been denied their true identities. The book depicts the poverty in which Malcolm grew up, his early bouts with authorities in social service agencies after his father was killed and his mother slowly losing her sanity, and his wild life on the streets of Detroit following his mother's institutionalization and the separation of his family. The street life led to his imprisonment, during which he was converted to the Muslim faith. He quickly became a respected leader in the Muslim community until his disagreements with Elijah Muhammad, head of the Black Muslims. The book ends shortly after he makes a trip to Mecca and begins to redefine his conception of whites as "devils."

The book was very well received and became required reading for many courses in colleges. It also had popular appeal; it was not uncommon to find young black men on street corners, in subways, or walking along the streets with copies of the book in their hands. The assassination of Malcolm X in 1965 contributed to the popularity of the book.

Writing Roots

Two weeks after he completed the manuscript for the book on Malcolm X, Haley wandered into the National Archives Building in Washington, D.C., to begin researching his own genealogy. At the time, Haley did not know that this initial search would eventually lead him to "50 or more archives, libraries and research repositories on three continents," before his curiosity would be satisfied, and that his efforts would culminate with the writing of *Roots*, published twelve years later on 1 October 1976.

Roots is the story of Kunta Kinte, a Mandinkan from the small village of Juffure Gambia in West Africa, and his American descendants; he was "the African" about whom Haley's grandmother and other relatives told stories. Haley imaginatively recreated his ancestor's life in Africa, his capture into slavery, and his experiences in the new world. Haley had been fascinated and intrigued by the story from childhood, because Kunta Kinte, he was told, refused to accept the ways and customs of his white masters and never forgot his African heritage. . . .

Alex Palmer Haley is the author of the 1965 best seller The Autobiography of Malcolm X.
AP Images.

Haley's grandmother, along with his aunts Viney, Mathilda, and Liz, perpetuated the traditional stories concerning the trials, tribulations, and successes of Kunta Kinte's family. Their front porch became their forum.

Hundreds of thousands of Americans identified vicariously with the story of *Roots* both in its book form and in the television adaptation. Haley himself continued the tradition of his family by sharing the stories with his own children, William, Lydia Ann, and Cindy.

Phenomenal Success

Although it took Haley twelve years to research and write *Roots*, it did not take nearly that long for it to reach the pinnacle of success. Two years following its publication, the book had won two hundred seventy-one awards, including a citation from the judges of the 1977 National Book Awards and the Pulitzer Prize. Within this short time, eight and one-half million copies of the book had been printed in twenty-six languages.

Much of the success of *Roots* can be attributed to the airing of two television mini-series which dramatically portrayed the saga outlined in the book. As a result of the television hit, *Roots* was one of the nonfiction best-sellers in 1977; it penetrated domestic, foreign, societal, cultural, geographical, racial, gender, age, and socioeconomic barriers with a laser effect. Of that effect, Paul Zimmerman wrote: "Instead of writing a scholarly monograph of little social impact, Haley has written a blockbuster in the best sense—a book that is bold in concept and ardent in execution, one that will reach millions of people and alter the way we see ourselves." Another testament to the phenomenon that *Roots* became is the fact that prior to the release of the book in paperback, it was used in two hundred seventy-six college courses.

The book was so broadly popular that a children's edition was published, as was a $75 special edition with gold trim.

Vernon Jordan, former director of the National Urban League, remarked in a *Time* magazine article that the televised version of *Roots* was "the single most spectacular educational experience in race relations in America."

This reaction was a surprise to the producers. Produced by David L. Wolper for ABC, *Roots* was originally planned to be televised over a much longer period of time, but was shown on eight consecutive nights due to an increased fear that it would be a monumental embarrassment. When the first part of the mini-series aired on 23 January 1977, it was universally acclaimed. Some one hundred thirty million Americans watched at least one of the episodes. Seven of the eight episodes ranked among the top ten shows in all TV ratings. At the end of its run, *Roots* had attained an average of 66 percent of the audience shares which had been projected at 31 percent; it was nominated for thirty-seven Emmy awards.

Roots was such a phenomenal success that ABC produced a sequel, *Roots: The Next Generation*. "Roots II," as it was called, cost $16.6 million to make and ran for fourteen hours. The first episode was aired on 18 February 1979. The story line began in 1882, twelve years after the end of "Roots I," and it ended in 1967.

During the eighty-five-year span of "Roots II" Haley's family was dramatized against the backdrop of the activities of the Ku Klux Klan, world wars, race riots, and the Great Depression. As one author notes, "Roots II" was also able to dramatize normal black middle-class life—at home, work, and college—and to show some of the heartbreaks, ambitions, and conflicts that blacks had in common with whites.

The Labors of Success

The *Roots* phenomenon turned Haley into an entrepreneur. He formed the Kinte Corporation in California and has become involved in the production of films and records. One of Haley's first productions was a record titled "Alex Haley

Speaks"; it features tips from Haley on how to research one's genealogy. Through such ventures, and others tied to the success of *Roots*, Haley has become a millionaire.

Haley's success has been marked by relentless hours of autographing tours and press interviews on radio and television, as well as in newspapers. Although he has also been on the lecture tour constantly, he has managed to find time to pursue other writing projects. . . .

Despite fame and fortune, Haley is rather restrained about his success. He commented: "The funny thing is that all that money has almost no meaning to me. I was broke so long that I got used to being without money. The few things I do want, including a decent stereo set, don't cost more than $5,000. All I'm concerned with is just being comfortable, being able to pay my debts, and having a little to buy something or make a gift to somebody."

Haley's success brought some conflicts in addition to the fortune. Amid his newly acquired wealth, he found himself involved in two plagiarism suits. The first was brought by Margaret Walker Alexander, author of *Jubilee* (1966), which had won the Houghton Mifflin Literary Fellowship Award; she charged Haley with copyright infringement on 20 April 1977. Eventually the charges were dropped, but not before Haley had incurred $100,000 in lawyers' fees. The second accusation of plagiarism was brought by Harold Courlander, author of *The African* (1968). Courlander claimed that certain passages in his book were plagiarized in *Roots*. On 14 December 1977, Haley conceded that the charge was accurate and paid $500,000 in out-of-court settlement fees; Courlander had sued for half the profits of *Roots*. According to Haley, "there were three paragraphs from [*The African*] that appeared verbatim in my notes." He explained that during the course of writing his book he often accepted undocumented notes and information from other people and (that some of what he used) "turned out to be extracted from Courlander's book."

Authenticity

Haley attempted to authenticate as much of the material in *Roots* as possible. He was so obsessed with authenticity, especially from the emotional perspective, that he went to extremes to validate his recreation of the emotional anguish that Kunta and others must have experienced on the middle passage. An *Ebony* interviewer recounted some of Haley's efforts: "He somehow scrounged up some money and flew to Liberia where he booked passage on the first U.S. bound ship. Once at sea, he spent the night lying on a board in the hold of the ship, stripped to his underwear to get a rough idea of what his African ancestor might have experienced. . . . That same night, he says, he went back into the hold. 'Lying again on that board, it was if some kind of catharsis had occurred. I felt for the first time that I was Kunta Kinte. From that moment on, I had no problem with writing what his senses had registered as he was crossing the ocean.'"

Through such meticulous attention to detail, Haley emerged as the first black American to trace his ancestry back to Africa, as documented by *Roots*. He is also admired by many for helping to foster better race relations. Hence, his indelible mark on history will not only be as a creative writer but as a great civil rights advocate. Haley bridged a part of the gap between the historical liaisons of Africans and Afro-Americans, and his name has become synonymous with the desire to know about heritage and roots. The book itself has been judged to be "an epic work destined to become a classic of American literature." [Alex Haley died of a heart attack on February 10, 1992, at the age of 70.]

Malcolm X as Spokesman and Leader

Bayard Rustin

Bayard Rustin played a pivotal role in the civil rights movement from the 1950s until his death in 1987. He served as an assistant to Martin Luther King, Jr., and headed the War Resisters' League.

Malcolm X's transformations—from white man's "mascot" to street hustler to prisoner to Nation of Islam leader—did not change his central identity. He was a man of intelligence, ambition, rebellion, and a desire for brotherhood and respectability. But the culmination of these traits contributed to his eventual conflict with other Muslim leaders. After breaking with the Nation of Islam, Malcolm did not easily find his place in the civil rights movement; some thought him too militant, others too moderate. Nonetheless, he made a substantial contribution to the movement, especially in his ability to offer hope to the poorest blacks.

This odyssey of an American Negro in search of his identity and place in society [*The Autobiography of Malcolm X*] really begins before his birth in Omaha, Neb. He was born Malcolm Little, the son of an educated mulatto West Indian mother and a father who was a Baptist minister on Sundays and dedicated organizer for Marcus Garvey's back-to-Africa movement the rest of the week.

The first incident Malcolm recounts, as if it were his welcome to white America, occurred just before he was born. A party of Ku Klux Klanners galloped up to his house, threatened his mother and left a warning for his father "to stop

Bayard Rustin, "Making His Mark: A Strong Diagnosis of America's Racial Sickness in One Negro's Odyssey," *Book Week–New York Herald Tribune*, November 14, 1965, pp. 1, 8, 10, 12, 16–17. Copyright © 1965 by The New York Times Company. Reproduced by permission.

spreading trouble among the good" Negroes and get out of town. They galloped into the night after smashing all the windows. A few years later the Klan was to make good on its threat by burning down the Littles' Lansing, Mich., home because Malcolm's father refused to become an Uncle Tom [a term that refers to a character in Harriet Beecher Stowe's, novel *Uncle Tom's Cabin*, who is represented as a black man submissive to whites]. These were the first in a series of incidents of racial violence, characteristic of that period, that were to haunt the nights of Malcolm and his family and hang like a pall over the lives of Negroes in the North and South. Five of Reverend Little's six brothers died by violence—four at the hands of white men, one by lynching, and one shot down by Northern police officers. When Malcolm was six, his father was found cut in two by a trolley car with his head bashed in. Malcolm's father had committed "suicide," the authorities said. Early in his life Malcolm concluded "that I too would die by violence. . . . I do not expect to live long enough to read this book."

The Limits Set by Race

Malcolm's early life in the Midwest was not wholly defined by race. Until he went to Boston when he was 14, after his mother suffered a mental breakdown from bringing up eight children alone, his friends were often white; there were few Negroes in the small Midwestern towns where he grew up. He recounts with pride how he was elected president of his eighth-grade class in an almost totally white school.

But the race problem was always there, although Malcolm, who was light-skinned, tried for a time to think of himself as white or just like anyone else. Even in his family life, color led to conflict that interfered with normal relationships. The Reverend Little was a fierce disciplinarian, but he never laid a hand on his light-skinned son because, unconsciously, according to Malcolm, he had developed respect for white skin. On the other hand, Malcolm's mother, whose father was a white man, was ashamed of this and favored Malcolm's darker brothers and sisters. Malcolm wrote that he spent his life trying to purge this tainted white blood of a rapist from his veins.

Race also set the limits on his youthful ambitions during what he describes as his "mascot years" in a detention home run by whites with mixed feelings of affection and superiority towards him. One of the top students in his school and a member of the debating club, Malcolm went to an English teacher he admired and told him of his ambition to become a lawyer. "Mr. Ostrowsky looked surprised and said, 'Malcolm, one of life's first needs is for us to be realistic . . . a lawyer, that's no realistic goal for a n----- . . . you're good with your hands . . . why don't you plan on carpentry?'" How many times has this scene been repeated in various forms in schoolrooms across the country? It was at this point, Malcolm writes, "that I began to change—inside. I drew away from white people."

Too many people want to believe that Malcolm "the angry black man sprang full grown from the bowels of the Harlem ghetto." These chapters on his childhood are essential reading for anyone who wants to understand the plight of American Negroes.

Learning to Hustle

Malcolm Little was 14 when he took the Greyhound to Boston to live with his half-sister, Ella, who had fought her way into the Boston "black bourgeoisie." The "400," as they were called, lived on "the Hill," only one step removed socially, economically and geographically from the ghetto ("the Town"). Malcolm writes that "a big percentage of the Hill dwellers were in Ella's category—Southern strivers and scramblers and West Indian Negroes, whom both the New Englanders and Southerners called 'Black Jews.'" Ella owned some real estate and her own home, and like the first Jews who arrived in the

New World, she was determined to shepherd new immigrants and teach them the strange ways of city life. There were deep bonds between Ella and her younger brother, and she tried to help him live a respectable life on the Hill.

But for Malcolm the 400 were only "a big-city version of those 'successful' Negro bootblacks and janitors back in Lansing . . . 8 out of 10 of the Hill Negroes of Roxbury . . . actually worked as menials and servants. . . . I don't know how many 40-and 50-year-old errand boys went down the Hill dressed as ambassadors in black suits and white collars to downtown jobs 'in government,' 'in finance,' or 'in law.'" Malcolm instead chose "the Town," where for the first time he felt he was part of a people.

Unlike the thousands of Negro migrants who poured into the Northern ghettos, Malcolm had a choice. But from the moment he made it, the options narrowed. He got a job at the Roseland Ballroom, where all the jazz greats played. His title was shoeshine boy but his real job was to hustle whiskey, prophylactics and women to Negroes and whites. He got his first conk and zoot suit and a new identity, "Red," and his secondary education began before he was 15. "I was . . . schooled well, by experts in such hustles as the numbers, pimping, con games of many kinds, peddling dope, and thievery of all sorts, including armed robbery."

It is significant that it was Malcolm's good qualities—his intelligence, integrity, and distaste for hypocrisy—as well as his sickness that made him choose crime rather than what passed in the Negro community for a respectable bourgeois life. Later he moved on to bigger things in Harlem, became "Detroit Red," went on dope and at one time carried three guns.

From Hustling to Prison

His description of the cutthroat competition between the hustlers and their fraternity is both frightening and moving. "As in the case of any jungle," he writes, "the hustler's every waking hour is lived with both the practical and the subconscious knowledge that if he ever relaxes, if he ever slows down, the other hungry, restless foxes, ferrets, wolves, and vultures out there with him won't hesitate to make him their prey." He summed up his morality at the time: "The only thing I considered wrong was what I got caught doing wrong . . . and everything I did was done by instinct to survive." As a "steerer" of uptown rich whites to Harlem "sex specialties," he recounts perversions with racial overtones, of white men begging to be beaten by black women or paying large amounts to witness interracial sex that make [playwright Jean] Genet's "The Balcony" [a play set in a brothel that catered to every man's fantasy] seem inhibited by comparison.

"Detroit Red" was a limited success in his trade for four years. But even in this business, success was limited by race. The big operators, the successful, respectable, and safe executives of policy, dope, and prostitution rackets, were white and lived outside the ghetto.

Malcolm left Harlem to return to Boston, and a few months later was caught as the head of a burglary gang. In February, 1946, not quite 21, he was sentenced to 10 years in prison, though the average sentence for burglary was about two years—the price for his being caught with his white girl friend and her sister.

Malcom's Religious Conversion

Most of the first year in prison, Malcolm writes, he spent in solitary confinement, cursing: "My favorite targets were the Bible and God." Malcolm got a new name from the other prisoners—"Satan"—and plenty of time to think. He went through what he described as a great spiritual crisis, and, as a result, he, the man who cursed God, bowed down and prayed to Allah. It will be difficult for those readers who have never been in prison to understand the psychological torment that prisoners experience, their feelings of isolation, their need to totally commit their minds to something outside of themselves. Men without any of the external economic symbols of status seek security in a religion, philosophy or ideology. Malcolm particularly, with his great feelings of rebelliousness, hatred and internal conflict, turned to books and ideas for relief. When his brothers and sisters wrote to him that they had become followers of Elijah Muhammad and sent him Elijah's teachings, Malcolm seized on the tracts. Stimulated, he read other books on religion and philosophy voraciously. In his spiritual and psychological crisis he underwent religious conversion.

He took on a new identity and became Malcolm X, a follower of Elijah Muhammad. Now he had a God to love and obey and a white devil responsible for his plight. Many Negro prisoners accepted the "Messenger," Elijah Muhammad, for similar reasons. Excluded from American society, they are drawn to another one, the Nation of Islam. (This analysis of why Malcolm joined the Muslims is mine, for although Malcolm writes about Muslim ideas, nowhere does he discuss the reasons for his conversion beyond a surface level.)

Out of prison, Malcolm, while remaining religious, arrived at a balanced view of the more fantastic elements of Elijah's teachings and a deeper understanding of one of the driving forces: "So many of the survivors whom I knew as tough hyenas and wolves of the streets in the old days now were so pitiful. They had known all the angles, but beneath that surface they were poor ignorant, untrained men; life had eased up on them and hyped them.... I was thankful to Allah that I had become a Muslim and escaped their fate."

Becoming Malcolm X

Alex Haley, who assisted Malcolm with [his autobiography], rightly commends him for deciding not to rewrite the first parts of the book and make it a polemic against his old leader

[Elijah Muhammad], although in the interim they had broken and now were in competition with each other. As a result the book interestingly shows changes in Malcolm's thinking.

After seven years in prison, Detroit Red emerged as Malcolm X and was soon to be the brightest star of the Nation of Islam. But as in every conversion, the man himself was not entirely reborn. Malcolm brought with him his traits of the past—the shrewd and competitive instincts learned on the ghetto streets, combined now with the language and thoughts of the great philosophers of Western culture he applied from reading [Georg] Hegel, [Immanuel] Kant, and [Friedrich] Nietzsche, and great Negro intellectuals like [W.E.B] Du Bois. Remaining, too, with his burning ambition to succeed, was the rebellious anger of his youth for being denied a place in society commensurate with his abilities. But on the other side of the coin was a desire for fraternity, family and respectability.

Because of his ability, he was sent to New York, where he struck a responsive chord with a great many Harlem Negroes. The Nationalist sects provided an arena of struggle for power and status denied lower-class Negroes in the outside world.

But the same qualities that made him a successful ghetto organizer soon brought him into conflict with other Muslim leaders, especially Elijah's children and prospective heirs. They saw Malcolm as a threat to their domain and apparently were able to convince Elijah that there was a threat to himself as well. For although Malcolm always gave corollary credit to Elijah—and the limits put upon him by Elijah's demands made many underestimate the exceptional nature of his mind—he could not totally constrain his brilliance, pride or ambition. "Only by being two people could I have worked harder in the service of the Nation of Islam. I had every gratification that I wanted. I had helped bring about the progress and additional impact such that none could call us liars when we called Mr. Muhammad the most powerful black man in America."

From Muhammad, to Mecca

As Malcolm's star rose higher in the western sky, Mr. Muhammad saw his eastern star setting and grew jealous. The conflict grew, although Malcolm made efforts toward conciliation. Finally, there was a total break that can be fatal to the erring Muslim who is cast away. Malcolm was aware of the dangers. "I hadn't hustled in the streets for nothing. I knew I was being set up ... As any official in the Nation of Islam would instantly have known, any death-talk for me could have been approved of—if not actually initiated—by only one man." Later, just before his death, Malcolm said the attempt to murder him would come from a much greater source than the Muslims: he never revealed about whom he was talking.

Under a death sentence and without money or any substantial organization, Malcolm opted for action, although it was unclear whether he was running away from or toward something as he began another phase of his odyssey—a pilgrimage to Mecca where he became El-Hajj Malik El-Shabazz. Throughout his many conversions and transformations, he never was more American than during his trip to Mecca. Because his ankles were not flexible enough, he was unable to sit properly cross-legged on the traditional Muslim rug with the others, and at first he shrank from reaching into the common food pot. Like many American tourists, he projected desires for hospitality and fraternity, frustrated at home, on the Muslims he met, most of whom he could not communicate with because of the language barrier. Back in America, he acknowledged that it would be a long time before the Negro was ready to make common struggle with the Africans and Arabs.

In Mecca, Malcolm also dramatically announced that he had changed his view on integration, because he had seen true brotherhood there between black and white Muslims. In reality he had begun changing his attitude on integration and the civil rights movement many months before as the divisions between him and Elijah Muhammad widened. Part-way through the book his attacks on the movement became muted, and in the epilogue Haley concludes that Malcolm "had a reluctant admiration for Dr. Martin Luther King."

Caught in a Trap

The roots of Malcolm's ambivalence were much more profound than personal opportunism. In a touching confession of dilemma he told Haley, "'the so-called moderate' civil rights organizations avoided him as 'too militant' and the 'so-called militants' avoided him as 'too moderate.' 'They won't let me turn the corner!' he once exclaimed. 'I'm caught in a trap!'" Malcolm was moving toward the mainstream of the civil rights movement when his life was cut short, but he still had quite a way to go. His anti-Semitic comments are a symptom of this malaise.

Had he been able to "turn the corner," he would have made an enormous contribution to the struggle for equal rights. As it was, his contribution was substantial. He brought hope and a measure of dignity to thousands of despairing ghetto Negroes. His "extremism" made the "mainstream" civil rights groups more respectable by comparison and helped them wrest substantial concessions from the power structure. Malcolm himself clearly understood the complicated role he played. At a Selma rally, while Dr. King was in jail, Malcolm said, "Whites better be glad Martin Luther King is rallying the people because other forces are waiting to take over if he fails." Of course, he never frightened the racists and the reactionaries as much as he made liberals feel uncomfortable, and moderates used his extremism as an excuse for inaction.

Behind the grim visage on television that upset so many white Americans there was a compassionate and often gentle man with a sense of humor. A testament to his personal honesty was that he died broke and money had to be raised for his funeral and family.

Upset by the comments in the African and Asian press criticizing the United States government for Malcolm's fate, Carl T. Rowan, Director of the United States Information Agency, held up some foreign papers and told a Washington audience, according to Alex Haley, ". . . All this about an ex-convict, ex-dope peddler, who became a racial fanatic." Yes, all this and more, before we can understand. Malcolm's autobiography, revealing little-known aspects of his life and character, makes that tortured journey more understandable.

Violence, Degradation, and Racism

Malcolm X

Much that has been written about Malcolm X has focused on his conversion to Islam, and especially the racist comments he made during and after this process. "The white man is the devil" is a much-repeated quotation of the man. In 1964, though, Malcolm X made a break with Elijah Muhammad and the Nation of Islam. A trip to Mecca opened his eyes to a world where people of all colors and ethnicities work together toward racial and social justice. At this moment, Malcolm began to believe in the possibility of integration. Admitting he was once a racist, Malcolm now wanted to work with both blacks and whites to "save America from a grave, possibly fatal catastrophe." The year after his break from the Nation of Islam, Malcolm X was assassinated by three members of the group.

No one needs to be reminded that on November 22, 1963, President John F. Kennedy was assassinated in Dallas, Tex. Within hours after the assassination every Muslim minister received a directive from Mr. Muhammad—to make no remarks at all concerning the assassination. I had a previously scheduled speaking engagement in New York at the Manhattan Center. It wasn't canceled, and the question-and-answer period, someone asked me right off the bat. "What do you think about President Kennedy's assassination?"

And I said without a second thought what I honestly felt—that, as I saw it, it was a case of "the chickens coming home to roost." I said that the hate in white men had not stopped with the killing of defenseless black people, but that, allowed to spread unchecked, it had struck this country's Chief of State. Black Muslims, Malcolm X! Chickens Come Home to Roost. That was promptly in headlines and on news broadcasts. The next day, I went to Chicago, on my monthly visit to Mr. Muhammad. "That was a very bad statement," he said. "The country loved this man. The whole country is in mourning. That was very ill-timed. A statement like that can make it hard on Muslims in general. I'll have to silence you for the next ninety days—so that the Muslims everywhere can be disassociated from the blunder."

I was numb. But I told Mr. Muhammad, "Sir, I agree with you, and I submit, one-hundred-percent."

When I got back to New York, prepared to tell my Mosque No. 7 assistants that I had been suspended, or, in my case, "silenced," I learned that already they had been informed. Next, an announcement was made that I would be reinstated within 90 days, "if he submits."

This made me suspicious for the first time. I had completely submitted. But Muslims were deliberately being given the implication that I had rebelled. Three days later the first word came to me that members of Mosque No. 7 were being told, "If you knew what the Minister did, you'd go out and kill him yourself." As a one-time hustler, I sensed that once again I had to leave town fast.

I remembered Cassius Clay. We met first in 1962 at a Detroit rally for Elijah Muhammad. Today he does not share my feelings about Mr. Muhammad. But I must always be grateful to him that just at this time, when he was training in Miami to fight Sonny Liston, he invited me, Betty and the children to come there, as his guests, as a sixth-wedding anniversary present to Betty and me. Miami was Betty's first vacation since we had married. And our girls loved the heavy-weight contender who romped and played with them. I was in a state of emotional shock. I made an error, I know now, in not speaking out the full truth when I was first "suspended."

What was I going to do? After the fight I returned to New, York City, where I had a large, direct personal following. Each day, more of the militant, "action" brothers who had been with me in Mosque No. 7 announced their automatically irrevocable break from the Nation of Islam to come with me.

The Hotel Theresa is at the corner of 125th Street and 7th Avenue, which might be called one of the fuse boxes of Harlem. I called a press conference and made the announcement: "I am going to organize and lead a new mosque in New York City known as the Muslim Mosque, Incorporated, with temporary headquarters in the Hotel Theresa. It will be the working base for an action program designed to eliminate the political oppression, the economic exploitation, and the social degradation suffered daily by twenty-two million Afro-Americans."

There was one major thing more that I needed to do. I took a plane, to my sister Ella, in Boston. "Ella," I said, "I want to make the pilgrimage to Mecca." Ella said, "How much do you need?"

I couldn't get over what she did then. I obtained a visa to the Holy City and I left New York quietly.

As a Muslim from America, I was the center of attention in Mecca. They asked me what about the Hajj had impressed me the most. I said, "The *brotherhood*: The people of *all* races, colors, from all over the world coming together as *one!* It has proved to me the power of the One God."

I never would have believed possible—it shocked me when I considered it—the impact of the Muslim World's influence on my previous thinking. Many blacks would cynically accuse me of "selling out" the fight, to become an "integrationist." Nearly all whites would scoff and jeer. But I knew that there were a few who would understand, who would accept, that in the land of Muhammad and Abraham, I had been blessed with a new insight into the religion of Islam.

Before I left the Holy City I had an audience with Prince Faisal, who encouraged me to bring the truth of Islam to American Negroes. I visited Nigeria and Ghana, where I talked with cabinet officers, intellectuals, ambassadors from the rest of Africa, and many others. Everywhere the reception for the militant American Muslim Negro was tremendous. In Dakar the Senegalese at the airport stood in line to shake my hand and ask for autographs.

From Dakar, I flew to Algiers. It was Tuesday, May 19, 1964—my birthday. It was 39 years since the scene of this book's beginning, with my mother pregnant with me standing on the porch in Nebraska, as the Ku Klux Klan threatened her.

My next plane, a Pan American jet—it was Flight 115—landed in New York on May 21 at 4:25 in the afternoon. As we left the plane and filed toward Customs, I saw the crowd—probably 50 or 60 reporters and photographers. Before any press queries could be made, I told of the alteration of my attitudes about white men who practiced *true* brotherhood, such as I had seen during my recent pilgrimage experience among Muslims in the Holy Land.

Over a hundred speaking invitations were waiting for me, either at home, or at the Muslim Mosque, Inc. In my busy weeks abroad I had had some chance to think about the basic types of white man in America, and how they affected Negro issues, and especially politics in this election year. I had thought out what I was going to say when I began appearing at some of these speaking engagements.

They call me sometimes "the angriest Negro in America." Well, the Bible says there is a *time* for anger. I feel that if Negroes attack white people, then those white people should defend themselves, with arms, if necessary, if the forces of law are inadequate. And I feel that Negroes, if white people attack them, should do exactly the same thing.

Johnson and Goldwater, I feel that as far as the American black man is concerned, are both just about the same. It's just a question of Johnson, the fox, or Goldwater, the wolf. "Conservatism" is only meaning "Let's keep the niggers in their place." and "Liberalism" is meaning "Let's keep the *knee*-grows in their place, but tell them we'll treat them a little better. Let's fool them more, with more promises." Since these are the choices, the black man in America, I think, only needs to pick which one he chooses to be eaten by, because they both will eat him.

Goldwater, I respect, as a man, because he speaks out his *convictions*. True convictions spoken out are rarely heard today in high-level politics. I think he's too intelligent to have risked his unpopular stand without conviction. He isn't another liberal just trying to please both racists and integrationists, smiling at one, and whispering to the other. Goldwater flatly tells the black man he's not for the black man. His policies make the black-white issue more clear-cut for the black man. So he makes the black man recognize what *he* has to do. The black man, if Goldwater would win, would realize that he had to fight harder; the black man would be more positive in his demands, more aggressive in his protests. The issue would he more quickly enjoined. While the black man under the liberal "fox" could keep on sitting around, begging and passive-resisting for another 100 years, waiting for "time" and for "good-will" to solve his problem.

The black man in America, when he awakens, when he becomes intellectually mature, when he becomes able to *think* for himself, then he will be able to make more independent choices.

I wouldn't put myself in the position of voting for either one, or of recommending to any black man to do so. I'm just talking about if America's white voters *do* install Goldwater, the black people will at least know what they are dealing with. They would at least know they were fighting an honestly growling wolf, rather than a fox who could have them in his stomach and half-digested before they even know what is happening.

They have called Goldwater a racist and me a racist. Once I was a racist—yes. But now, I have turned my direction away from anything that's racist. So, some of the followers of Elijah Muhammad would still consider it a first-rank honor to kill me. Also I know that any day, any night, I could die at the hands of some white devil racists. At the same time, however, I can't think of any subject involving human beings today that you can divorce from the race issue. I will even go so far as to say that I dream that one day history will look upon me as having been one of the voices that perhaps helped to save America from a grave, even possibly fatal catastrophe. If the reader can understand me, if then he can multiply me by the tens of thousands, he will put down this life story with at least a better picture than he had of America's black ghettoes.

More and worse riots will erupt. The black man has seen the white man's underbelly of guilty fear. But, if through telling this story of my life, I have brought any light, if I have spread any truth then all of the credit is due to Allah. Only the mistakes have been mine.

CHAPTER 2

The Autobiography of Malcolm X and Racism

Racist Violence

Samuel A. Weiss

Samuel A. Weiss, editor of Drama in the Modern World *(1974), taught literature at the University of Illinois.*

Before Malcolm X was even born, racism was a controlling factor in his life. In reaction to the racist violence endured by his family and so many other black families of his time, Malcolm spent 12 years preaching that all whites were devils, urging blacks to embrace racial separation, not integration. Not until his trip to Mecca in 1964 did Malcolm begin to believe in a world where blacks and whites together could fight for racial justice. But the following year he was killed by Nation of Islam members. Through his death, Malcolm became a martyr, and his influence became even greater.

Violence enveloped the man. While Malcolm was still in the womb, night riders attacked his family home; his earliest vivid memory was of another home being burned to the ground by marauding whites; his *Autobiography* ends with solemn previsions of his murder. Between birth and early death—he was about forty—he packed an extraordinary lifetime of experience, sordid and exalting, debased and purified, intense, exciting, and breathlessly active. Ever expecting sudden, violent death, he lived toward the end on borrowed time. Hardly sleeping, always on the go, organizing, preaching, debating, living by his watch, snatching every free moment to read or check some fact, intense, restless, electrifying. A black panther. Negro moderates feared and avoided him, Negro artists idolized him, the black Harlem masses trusted him. "Liberals" of both colors denounced him as an irresponsible racist and fomenter of violence. Yet he never led a violent demonstration; in fact, for the major part of his ministry he and his followers were aloof from the civil rights struggle.

He was unmistakably an American product, an anguished native son exposing the racist American cancer, casting the guilt of white America before it and arousing its deepest fears for the security of its civilization and privileged well-being. For twelve years he taught the Negro not to love the white man but to see in him the devil incarnate. He derided pie-in-the-sky religion for the black man, while white Christians enjoyed their heaven on earth. Look at your surroundings, he urged his listeners, and then look at the white man's, and you'll see what Christianity really means.

He counseled racial separation and scorned "integration-mad" Negroes for wanting to escape their own people. Physically and spiritually he was of the ghetto and worked to awaken "brain washed" Negroes to their bitter history of enslavement, abuse, exploitation, and brutalization, robbed of their native identities and languages and reduced to self-doubt, self-hate, passivity, ignorance, poverty, vice, and crime. He was born Malcolm Little. In protest against destruction of black tribal identity he called himself Malcolm X.

Defying Stereotypes

His second passion was to confront the white man with his crimes against non-whites, the greatest, he claimed, in history. Yet the white man, as colonizer, slavemaster, imperialist, and racist, remained smugly assured of his moral, intellectual, and human superiority. So deep is the racist rot in the American soul that it is unthinkable, Malcolm argued, that more than a tiny fraction of whites will tolerate integration with Negroes. Nor do the black masses wish integration. Like all nations and peoples they wish to preserve their identity and integrity.

He raged against the white man's blood—"that white rapist"—in his veins and taunted Negroes who thought light color superior, who cooked their hair in lye to remove its Negro features, who preferred white women and mimicked white tastes and fashions, who wasted money seeking acceptance in white establishments while the black ghetto starved for funds. He cried out in pity and anger at the slum jungles in the North, ridden with hustlers, pimps, prostitutes, alcoholics, and junkies, surrounded by rejecting and suspicious white communities, and policed by unsympathetic and domineering cops. He demanded of the Negro self-respect, self-help, discipline, dignity, and pride, and his Muslim creed was sternly puritanic: no illicit sex, intoxicants, cigarettes, pork, movies, or dancing.

Many Negroes, otherwise attracted, were repelled by the strict Muslim code. Intellectuals might dismiss it as middle-class morality. But Islamic stress on chastity, family purity, respect for women, the patriarchal role of husband as head and protector of the family rehabilitated black manhood and family stability undermined by generations of slavery, discrimination, and economic insecurity. Muslims were to be the opposite of the Negro stereotype: neatly dressed, immaculately clean, chaste, abstemious, independent, hardworking, dignified, protective of their women and families, proud of their color and natural features. They were not to be aggressors but if attacked were not to turn the other cheek. Muslims did not love "the enemy" but their brothers and in the fraternal cult found a warmth and belongingness that overcame the alienation and stark survival struggle of the ghetto.

Mental and Moral Support

But there were rumors of "blood brothers," judo practice, comments about rifle clubs, accusations of reverse racism, black supremacy goals, incitement to hate and violence. Malcolm did propagate the fantastic [Muslim] myth of the evil magician, Yacub, who bred a bleached-out race of white men from the original black man. He did identify the white man as the devil whose baleful reign over the oppressed black man was nearing its close. And he preached separation, not integration. But to distort this doctrine into a real threat of black supremacy in which the power of the races would be reversed and Negroes subjugate the overwhelming white majority is paranoid delusion, even as labeling Malcolm a racist hate-monger was superficial and hypocritical.

What Malcolm taught was not control of Negroes over whites nor continuation of present segregation but the voluntary separation of the Negro community from surrounding white corruption; not submission to imposed segregation that assumes Negro inferiority but the conscious reconstruction of an independent, self-reliant black community with its own identity, culture, economy, and political structure situated on its own land. He encouraged race pride by detaching the Negro from psychological dependence on whites and their emasculating image of him. He exposed Christian pretenses and asked his hearers how they could worship a blond, blue-eyed god that did not even look like them or be deceived by doctrines of brotherly love taught by those who do not even allow Negroes into their churches. The logic is faulty, but the *psycho*-logic is powerful.

Malcolm hammered at the Negro's shameful surrender of self-respect in adopting the ideology of his oppressors and of those who despise him. Instead he offered Islam associated with Africa and millions of dark-skinned believers. At one stroke the Muslim convert became special; Islamic prohibitions strengthened self-discipline and lent a new sense of worth. To the Negro daily exposed to the ravages of dope and alcohol, vice and crime, strict Muslim morality signified salvation from the gutter. Patriarchal teachings on male-female relations repaired damaged masculinity; injunctions to work and self-reliance kept the Muslim from demoralizing idleness and parasitism. Myths about the original black man, his great civilizations and oppression by a devil race whose days were

A young Malcolm X displays a newspaper discussing freedom in the early 1960s. For twelve years, Malcolm preached that all whites were devils, urging blacks to embrace racial separation, not integration. It wasn't until his 1964 trip to Mecca that Malcolm began to believe in a world where blacks and whites could join in the fight for racial justice. AP Images.

numbered enhanced self-acceptance. And money that previously might go for gambling, drink, sex, and dope was now available for constructive joint enterprises.

The Negro who believed that he descended from a great people with a great past and greater future that temporarily were subjugated by a devil race could not regard his racial fate as a curse. Identifying "Whitey" as the devil discouraged *Uncle Tomming* [named after the main character in Harriet Beecher Stowe's novel *Uncle Tom's Cabin*, the phrase refers to blacks who do anything to please white people, even betray their "own" people], and betrayal of Negro interests to white susceptibilities. Little wonder the Nation of Islam appealed most to the deprived, lower-class Negro, who desperately needed its mental and moral support. (Muslims had exceptional success in reclaiming addicts and convicts. To hold this against them is strange in those who profess the sanctity of repentance.)....

The White Devil Myth

By identifying the white man as devil, Malcolm directly clashed with the established Negro leadership whose co-operation with whites in common undertakings for Negro social reform was integral to their ideology and organization. Boards of "progress" organizations had whites as well as Negroes; money was largely derived from white contributions through foundations or private philanthropy. Inevitably white opinion had great influence on the policies of the organizations. Malcolm dismissed these organizations as Negro fronts for white control of the civil rights movement that hobbled militancy. He ridiculed the March on Washington as a farce cleverly manipulated by liberal whites and government persons with the co-operation of Negro "leaders" to gut the spontaneous protest that initiated the march. For the white man who demanded love, Malcolm had the retort that the white man was in no moral position to denounce hatred so long as he was guilty of despising and exploiting non-whites. The rapist, he cried, doesn't ask the person raped, do you love me. "Why, when all my ancestors are snake-bitten, and I'm snake-bitten, and I warn my children to avoid snakes, what does that *snake* sound like accusing *me* of hate-teaching?"

By attacking the historical guilt of the white community toward the Negro, Malcolm tapped ghetto tensions and gave them expression. The deprived slum Negro had only to look about him to discover hell and the rule of devils. The danger, I believe, was not so much incitement to ineffectual violence—his attacks may even have purged some poison from his followers' burdened psyches—as providing scapegoats to divert attention from the Negro's implication in his condition. This danger of non-critical self-pity the Muslims counteracted by insisting that the Negro resist demoralization and the vices spawned in the white-imposed slum jungle. "Kick Whitey off your back," the writhing addict would be urged, and the enemy within became an objective symbol that must and could be overcome.

In fact, the white devil myth spread by Malcolm was largely abstract. Of his personal vehemence, distrust, and restless anger there is no question. For the largest part of his ministry he condemned the white man outright, admitting of no exceptions and rejecting all gratitude for advances made. "Four hundred years the white man has had his foot-long knife in the black man's back—and now the white man starts to *wiggle* the knife out, maybe six inches! The black man's supposed to be *grateful*? Why, if the white man jerked the knife *out*, it's still going to leave a *scar*!" The greatest miracle achieved by Christian America was keeping millions of Negroes, under inhuman conditions, so peaceful so long. Malcolm would not concede an inch to his opponents, but endlessly attacked the chinks in their armor, evaded their thrusts, and demolished their defenses in an irresistible drive against white arrogance, smugness, hypocrisy, and exploitation. . . .

Malcolm's version of his crucial split with Elijah Muhammad [in 1964] needs corroborative evidence. But the *Autobiography* as narrated to Alex Haley breathes with such transparent honesty that one never suspects Malcolm of deception. Yet he could be wrong about himself and others. He may not have seen deeply enough his messianic-martyr drives; he may well have unconsciously wished to supplant Elijah Muhammad. (One of the most impressive qualities of the *Autobiography*, however, is Malcolm's personal modesty; there is quiet pride in what he achieved against enormous odds, but no bragging or self-importance; in a genuine way he appears humble.) His attacks on whites, correct in essence, were still one-sided, as were his criticisms of Jews: Jews were prominent in civil rights activities but their secret motive was to divert prejudice from themselves! Malcolm appreciated people's desire for cultural identity on a stable base, but he could see only hypocrisy in Jews moving out of decaying, transitional neighborhoods. Jewish ownership of stores in the black ghettoes, a holdover from days when the neighborhoods were Jewish, outraged him, as did the sale of gaudy junk at high credit rates; but he said nothing about credit risks. Racial groups, not an evil system, were at fault. Malcolm never completely overcame his deep distrust of people. And only toward the end of his life did he concede the possibility of some whites being genuinely sincere. By then he was moving toward deeper and broader visions and revising earlier positions. The change came with his pilgrimage to Mecca.

The Possibility of Universal Brotherhood

In Mecca Malcolm saw a gathering of all races and colors in common worship of Allah. He was profoundly moved by the hospitality he received from white-skinned Arab dignitaries. (He apparently discounted that they might have had their own political motives for being interested in spreading Islam among American Negroes.) The result for Malcolm was a tempered humanitarian position that accepted the ideal of universal brotherhood and jettisoned [omitted] the image of the white devil. Shared belief in one God and one mankind could effect racial harmony; he had seen it. But under the aegis [protection] of Allah. Christianity had failed; Islam could succeed. But the immediate problem for the American Negro was to rehabilitate his self-respect, and this demanded a separate identity in an autonomous community capable of self-help and morally supported by the colored nations of Africa. Black nationalism was therefore a necessary prelude to eventual black-white reconciliation. And the issue was human rights, not civil rights. As for the American white, he was not inherently evil but the victim of a corrupting environment and in need of stern atonement. For that he had to recognize his guilt.

Malcolm continued to grow. After a discussion with a white Algerian revolutionary, he re-examined the very term *black nationalism* and found it too narrowly and racially conceived. He seems even to have finally accepted intermarriage as a private matter. He was groping toward wider goals and new activities and saw the American Negro's struggle as part of an international movement by non-whites for liberation and requiring thorough social renovation. But he was no revolutionary theorist offering a many-sided, coherent analysis of Negro-white relations, their major and subsidiary conflicts, class composition, economic motives, stages of development within the Negro movement, need for internal unity and external allies, avoidance of sectarianism, and so on. He sorely needed an effective organization and concrete activist program.

Meanwhile, Malcolm continued to shock his white interlocutors with militant replies: he called for active self-defense and spoke of sending guerillas into Mississippi (which he defined as anywhere below the Canadian border). But his spirit seemed to flag. The price he paid for twelve years of blind fealty [loyalty] to Elijah Muhammad weighed heavily; the loss of the Nation of Islam, which he above anyone built to national prominence, was an unhealed wound; he expected death momentarily. The police thought Malcolm was bluffing when he said assassins were hunting him. He was right in thinking that he would not live to see his book into print.

Achieving Martyrdom

With his death, Malcolm achieved his martyrdom. Never has his influence seemed greater. While "white power" moves sluggishly and half-heartedly toward relieving the packed tensions of its cities and is unable or unwilling to grant the Negro his just share of economic, political, and social power, the dominantly middle-class articulation of Negro needs, stressing integration of schooling and housing, is increasingly challenged by the cry of Black Power from those militants identifying with the depressed Negro masses and demanding, not integration, but viable independent black communities backed by political power. (How these autonomous enclaves will solve the staggering economic problems of the Negro they have yet to explain.) They speak of self-defense and the role of force in effecting social change. Their inspiration is Malcolm X, whose spirit haunts America.

> Yes, I have cherished my "demagogue" role. I know that societies have killed the people who have helped to change those societies. And if I can die having brought any light, having exposed any meaningful truth that will help to destroy the racist cancer that is malignant in the body of America—then, all of the credit is due to Allah. Only the mistakes have been mine.

More long, hot summers are to come, and the voice of the ghetto will be heard throughout the land. So long as white power groups, out of fear, ignorance, or prejudice, continue to ignore or evade it, the ghost of Malcolm X will not be laid to rest.

The Psychological Impact of Racism

David Polizzi

David Polizzi is a faculty member of the department of criminology and criminal justice at Indiana State University.

David Polizzi argues that, in his autobiography, Malcolm X analyzes the complicated psychological impact of racism on blacks. At age 15, Malcolm discovered a reality he never could have imagined. Moving from Lansing, Michigan, to Boston to live with his half-sister Ella, he watched blacks behave in a way he had not witnessed in Lansing. Ella lived in Roxbury, which Malcolm described as "the snooty black neighborhood." It hadn't taken him long to find fault with the Roxbury blacks. He believed that in their attempts to improve their economic and social situations, they looked down on other blacks and thus rejected their own blackness, perpetuating a psychology of self-hatred.

After completing the eighth grade, Malcolm left Lansing, Michigan to live in Boston with his [half]-sister Ella, who had arranged to be granted official custody of him. Malcolm states that "No physical move in my life has been more pivotal or profound in its repercussions." He reflects that if he had remained in Lansing, he probably would have married, taken one of the many menial jobs allotted to blacks in those days, and thought himself a success. Malcolm sees his move from Lansing as signifying much more then merely a geographic relocation. [His] relocation represents a movement away from a particular understanding of black experience that is overly circumscribed by the demands of [racists]. Within this context ... success becomes defined through the black individual's willingness to accept this menial status in white society. Ultimately, this notion of relocation comes to signify a relocation of meaning and possibility for black-being-in-the-world whose validity is not contingent upon how white society comes to define black success.

Black Rejection of Blackness

Malcolm provides a clear example of this observation:

> I've often thought that if Mr. Ostrowski had encouraged me to become a lawyer, I would today probably be among some city's black bourgeoisie, sipping cocktails and palming myself off as a community spokesman for and leader of the suffering black masses, while my primary concern would be to grab a few more crumbs from the groaning board of the two-faced whites with whom they're begging to integrate.

Here, professional status does not necessarily become proof of success in an authentic way if success is somehow valued as an acceptance of the white status quo. Malcolm rejects all possibilities for black-being-in-the-world that are overly circumscribed by the demands of white society and which by their very nature, demand a rejection of blackness. Malcolm's departure from Michigan, then, not only represents an end to a particular style of being-in-the-world, it also represents his attempt to discover other possibilities for black experience that his past life in Lansing could not provide.

A High Price for "Success"

Upon arriving in Boston, Malcolm is surprised by the attitudes of some blacks he encounters in his new neighborhood:

> I saw those Roxbury Negroes acting and living differently from any black people I'd ever dreamed of in my life. This

was the snooty-black neighborhood; they called themselves the Four Hundred, and they looked down their noses at the Negroes of the black ghetto.

Malcolm assumed that these individuals must be highly successful, well educated and living important lives. When he realizes that most of these individuals worked as "menials or servants," he states that what he was really seeing was "the big-city version of those successful Negro bootblacks and janitors back in Lansing." . . .

Malcolm's surprise at seeing blacks "acting and living differently" from any blacks he had known in Lansing represents a momentary challenge to his understanding of black possibility and becomes a direct contradiction to his actual experience. What seems to challenge his understanding of the "Roxbury Negroes" most is realizing that their material situation is clearly better than all of the blacks he knew in Lansing, which, in turn, no doubt raised his own expectations concerning what would be possible for him in Boston. Though Malcolm states that these individuals appear to equate their material well being with being like whites, and thereby using this yardstick as indicative of the measure of black success, his impression is that they fail to understand just how high a price is being paid in this transaction. . . .

Black Self-Deception

[The] attitude of superiority which Malcolm experiences from these individuals is almost defensive in nature. Their "status," rather than signifying any real accomplishment of success, represents a disburdening of the everyday reality of racism through the fabrication of a lie that allows them to believe they have risen above the menial status of most other blacks, therefore, making them better, making them closer to white.

However, as Malcolm points out, this self-deception does little more than [numb] them against the effects of racism and even the realities of class inequality present in American society as well. It could be argued that the desire of these African-Americans to live better than other blacks is predicated more on the dynamics of a capitalist fantasy, which seems to equate material affluence with human worth, than it is the "brainwashing effects of racism." One could even argue that the haughty behavior Malcolm is so surprised by becomes an attempt by these individuals to construct an image of themselves that the reality of their economic position would seem to contradict. Such accounts, however, still do not sufficiently explain the presence of black self-loathing that Malcolm attributes to the reality of racism. . . .

The Black Other

Lewis Gordon, in his text *Bad Faith and Antiblack Racism*, discusses [the] notion of self-hatred within the context of what he calls "Black Antiblackness in an Antiblack World:"

> The "other black" must be punished at all costs because he carries in his gaze a powerful truth. A lone black in a room of whites *sees* only white people. He is able to live deluded in the belief that if he cannot see his black skin then it is no longer black but transformed and coordinated with his white mask. He is *seduced* by the situation. He lives a deluded "we."

The truth Gordon situates in the black other is the truth of racism and the meaning for blackness this truth imposes on all those who are seen as black. The seduction Gordon describes is the momentary reprieve that the absence of the black other provides for those attempting to escape the implications of their blackness in a racist society: I will not be reminded of my blackness, and, therefore will believe that I will be allowed to be like others, how white others, are allowed to be. As Gordon states, this is delusional in an antiblack world insofar as nothing has actually been transformed concerning the meaning of blackness. Though the absence of the black

A close-up of the typewritten manuscript of Alex Haley's The Autobiography of Malcolm X, *with handwritten notes and comments by Haley.* Time & Life Pictures/Getty Images.

other allows me to forget my own blackness, it remains vividly present to those who are not black that I am not like them.

Rejecting Roxbury, Embracing Blackness

A similar type of delusion takes place through the perception Malcolm has of the "Roxbury Negroes" whose perspective appears to be, "if I don't live like other blacks, then I am not black." Here, the possibility for seduction is constructed not by the absence of the "black other" but through the presence of a privileged economic status which the "black other" does not possess. The psychological distancing between the Roxbury Negroes and other poorer blacks, as witnessed by Malcolm, is their attempt to distance themselves from the image of blackness which [racists have] constructed. Much like the individual in Gordon's account, the racist meaning for blackness remains, and is, in fact, affirmed through the actions of these individuals. Malcolm ultimately refuses to take his sister's advice concerning his involvement with blacks in the more af fluent sections of Roxbury and becomes more attracted to the ghetto section of his neighborhood:

> I felt more relaxed among Negroes who were being their natural selves and not putting on airs. Even though I did live on the Hill, my instincts were never—and still aren't—to feel myself any better than any other Negro.

Malcolm seems to be able to make this statement because he does not get taken in by the false belief that personal wealth is the yardstick by which to measure human worth. More to the point, he refuses to take an antiblack stance against other blacks because he realizes that not only does such a stance demand the rejection of blackness, it is also hopelessly intoxicated by the false promise of white acceptance. What Malcolm finally rejects is not the possibility of black affluence, but a specific psychological attitude evoked by a peculiar relationship to material wealth.

Black Identity Shaped by White Racism

John Barresi

John Barresi is a psychology professor at Dalhousie University in Halifax, Nova Scotia. In 2007 he published Understanding Intentional Relations of Self and Other.

As a child Malcolm X abandoned his black identity in an attempt "to become white." His belief that he could so easily "fit in" diminished the moment his eighth-grade English teacher told him his aspiration to become a lawyer was impractical because he was black. This marked what Malcolm referred to as "the first major turning point" in his life. Shortly after, when he moved to Boston to live with his half-sister, Malcolm embraced the identity of ghetto hustler. This lifestyle brought him to New York, and then to prison, where yet another identity arose. In prison Malcolm embraced faith in Allah, belief in black supremacy, and a view of whites as "devils." He would carry the latter belief for the next 12 years.

Malcolm's earliest vivid nightmare memory was of when his family's house was set on fire while they were in it asleep at night. Malcolm was 4 years old at the time. Two years later, in 1931, his father was likely killed by the same racist group by being placed, unconscious, under a trolley. Malcolm viewed both of these events as examples of White hatred directed at his family. But in his account, he saw his family as a victim of White racism in America that was more general than these overt acts of hatred. For instance, when his father died only one insurance policy on his life paid its premium; the company of the second larger one declared that his

John Barresi, *Identity and Story: Creating Self in Narratives.* Washington, DC: American Psychological Association Press, 2006. Reproduced by permission.

father committed suicide. Then, during the Depression years, when his family was in poverty and Malcolm got in trouble for stealing food, the officials from the state social services agency, rather than helping the family hold itself together, broke it up by placing Malcolm and some of the other children in foster homes. A major result was that his mother's spirit was beaten. Her sense of independence and racial pride was defeated by the system of institutionalized White racism, and she retreated into mental illness. She was placed in a mental institution by the authorities, and the family became disconnected.

"Trying to Be White"

After getting into additional trouble at school Malcolm was eventually placed in a detention center run by a White couple, who took a liking to him and whom, in turn, Malcolm tried to please. In the process, Malcolm surrendered his Black identity and tried to "become" White.... In an attempt to forget his traumatic past and living in a congenial White environment, Malcolm attempted to place a White "mask" on his Black skin, trying to fit in White society in whatever way they would accept him, while at the same time half believing that this same society would never think of him as more than an inferior being, a "mascot" or "thing." By the time that he was elected president of his otherwise all-White seventh-grade class, he had become deluded by his apparent success, both in academics and popularity: "I was proud [of being elected]. I'm not going to say I wasn't. In fact, by then, I didn't really have much feeling about being a Negro, because I was trying so hard, in every way I could, to be white."

But this source of pride in his new "personal identity" did not last long. Within a year, his deluded sense of White success became unmasked by his English teacher. Mr. Ostrowski's response to Malcolm's comment that he would like to become a lawyer shattered forever Malcolm's belief that Black Americans could ever "become" White or successfully integrate with Whites on an equal basis in the United States.

> Mr. Ostrowski looked surprised. . . . He kind of smiled and said, "Malcolm, one of life's first needs is to be realistic. Don't misunderstand me now. We all here like you, you know that. But you've got to be realistic about being a n-----. A lawyer—that's no realistic goal for a n-----. You need to think about something you *can* be. You're good with your hands—making things. . . . Why don't you plan on carpentry?"

A Turning Point

With the illusion of becoming White shattered, believing that his own intellectual ability and accomplishments did not matter and that what did matter was that he was Black, Malcolm lost interest in school and wanted to leave the White world he was living in. In his autobiography he described this event as "the first major turning point in my life."

Fortunately, during this same period his half-sister, Ella, a daughter from his father's first marriage, visited Malcolm's family from Boston. He was extremely impressed with her.

> I think the major impact of Ella's arrival, at least upon me, was that she was the first really proud black woman I had ever seen in my life. She was mainly proud of her very black skin. This was unheard of among Negroes in those days, especially in Lansing.

It is interesting to note that it is shortly after mentioning that his family no longer talked about his institutionalized mother, whose Black pride had been broken by White racism, that Ella is described as the "first really proud black woman" he ever saw. In any event, the die was cast, and a turning point reached in Malcolm's first attempt, at 13, to form a personal identity. Although he reported that his remark about becoming a lawyer was not made in any seriousness, his teacher's response put an end to any attempt to find a personal identity in a White cultural context. Then the appearance of Ella on the scene provided him with a possible alternative—to move to Boston and live with her in a wholly Black community, something he may have dreamed of doing, when, as a child, he first saw pictures of Garveyites [followers of black leader Marcus Garvey, who preached that blacks should return to their African homes] parading in a wholly Black crowd. In a short while, he was able to arrange the move to join Ella. This move changed the direction of his life in a radical manner.

Still, we should not sell short what Malcolm learned about White Americans during his time living with them. He got to know how they thought about Negroes. He also learned how to succeed in social contexts with them. Unlike many Blacks raised in central-city ghettos, where Malcolm would later come to live and eventually thrive, he, early in his life, was exposed to the White culture and even seemed to succeed for a while within that context. But he learned the distinction between being White and being Black among Whites. However friendly Whites were to him, there was always an undercurrent of superiority in their interactions with him. He was never really accepted as an equal, so, despite any success he achieved, he could never, once disillusionment set in, really trust White America to overcome its racist attitudes. This early experience conditioned his later skepticism about integration, while also rendering him capable of communicating face to face with White people.

Negative Identity

The next phase of Malcolm's life [involved] a negative identity—that of a hustler in the ghettos of Boston and New York. This period began when he moved in with his half-sister in Boston and almost immediately got involved in hustler activities. School no longer had any interest for him, and becoming a member of the Negro middle-class, which he equated to striving to fit into White America, seemed to him a sham. He judged it better to be Black among Blacks and to steep oneself into ghetto life. But in entering that life, he adopted an identity that [psychologist Erik] Erikson called a negative identity. Such an identity glorifies what would otherwise appear negative. The life of a hustler was the negative projection of the White American ideal—at least, so it seems from the point of view of that ideal. But, on the other hand, the ghetto also provided a field of activity in which Malcolm could acquire a personal identity and become a success, where he could receive the respect of at least some of his Black peers. The ghetto also included a positive cultural side for Black Americans, in music and dancing and in creative writing, all of which Malcolm would participate in at one time or another during his life. Moreover, the northern Black ghettos were a hotbed for Black nationalist philosophy, which would become significant for Malcolm's later development.

As the older and wiser Malcolm looked back on his hustler years, especially at the first "conking" of his hair, and the self-infliction of so much pain to make his hair look straight like a White man's, he said that it was his "first really big step toward self-degradation." Malcolm's retrospective attitude about his ghetto existence as a hustler was that he was living at "dead level"—not really being alive, although obviously thinking at the time that he was. He realized that the roles he played as hustler fed the sickness that was White America, where, on the one hand, White people pretended to live honorable lives among other Whites, while, on the other hand, they sought out the excitement of sex, music, drugs, gambling, and so forth in the central city ghettos, where they forced Black people to live and expected them to provide these activities. Some Black people, including hustlers such as Malcolm, fed these desires. Harlem, particularly early on, was a thriving culture, because dance music, liquor, drugs, and sex were all readily available, with few questions asked, and little interference by police, who were happy to be paid off and to allow these activities to occur in Black rather than in their own White neighborhoods.

In Malcolm's case, he rose eventually from a shoe-shine boy, selling drugs, and so forth, in Boston to become a gun-toting hustler in Harlem, who managed women and steered White men to whatever sexual activities suited their desires. At first, he was careful in his own use of drugs, but eventually became addicted. As a hustler with a gun, he also came into conflict with other hustlers, and came close to a showdown with another New York hustler, before escaping to Boston. In Boston he organized a burglary gang, which included his long-time White mistress Sophia. He was eventually caught when he tried to pick up a stolen watch that he was having repaired. [in *Malcolm: The Life of a Man Who Changed Black America*, Bruce] Perry suggested that Malcolm unconsciously got himself caught at that time because he realized that his hustling career had failed, and he needed a way to escape it. In any event, probably because he was a Black man with a White mistress, he was sentenced to 8 to 10 years in prison for a relatively minor crime. He was 20 years old at the time.

Transformations in Prison

Malcolm's 6-year term in prison (he was paroled before his full sentence was served) was, in terms of the development of personal identity, the most important period of his life. It was the time when he recreated himself from a minor hoodlum, with addictions, virtually no education, and a self-defeating attitude toward life, into a self-educated, religious believer, with a self-confident, optimistic, and morally upright attitude toward life. He also acquired, through his new religion, a mission to teach other Black people how to get rid of their own negative identities, as he had his. Part of that lesson was for them to realize that the main cause for their negative lifestyle was the "White devil." However, Malcolm's stay in prison involved much more than a religious conversion to the Nation of Islam. Even before he heard about the Black Muslims from other family members, he was already undergoing transformations in prison. As detailed in his autobiography, it was mainly under the mentorship of a wise older Black prisoner named Bimbi that he awoke to the futility of his self-destructive behavior. Bimbi recognized that Malcolm had misdirected intellectual capacities, and he taught him how to regain their rightful use. Malcolm began a program of self-education that, once combined with his interest in the dogma and mythology of the Nation of Islam, led him in directions of self-reflection about Blacks and Whites in America, which would eventually result in a major transformation not only in Malcolm's self-narrative but in the self-narratives of many Black Americans.

From the point of view of theory, what is fascinating about Malcolm's psychosocial moratorium in prison, and his arrival at a new personal identity during that time, is how such a radical transformation could occur. When he entered prison his attitude was self-defeating: He was still on drugs, constantly in solitary for breaking rules, and always swearing against God and religion. Because of this behavior he was called "Satan" by other inmates. Yet, in his transformation, this self-hatred and anger with God eventually reversed itself into a hatred of a different source—the "White devil," or White race, which in the origin myth of the Nation of Islam were all created as devils. And, instead of anger with God and religion, he converted to the Nation of Islam and loved Allah.

Two Selves

Malcolm's description of his conversion well illustrates the dialogical nature of self in transformation. . . . Malcolm was aware of two selves within himself, the "bad" satanic self he had been and the "good" religious self he ultimately became. The dialogical struggle between these two selves was most intense in his attempt to pray.

The hardest test I ever faced in my life was praying. You understand. My comprehending, my believing the teachings of Mr. Muhammad [Elijah Muhammad, head of the Nation of Islam] had only required my mind's saying to me, "That's right!" Or, "I never thought of that."

But bending my knees to pray—that *act*—well, that took me a week. . . .

I had to force myself to bend my knees. And waves of shame and embarrassment would force me back up.

For evil to bend its knees, admitting its guilt, to implore the forgiveness of God, is the hardest thing in the world. It's easy for me to say that now. But, then, when I was the personification of evil, I was going through it.

Nevertheless, after repeated struggles to kneel and pray, he did succeed, and soon he was into his new character and life.

I still marvel at how swiftly my previous life's thinking pattern slid away from me, like snow off a roof. It is as though someone else I knew of had lived by hustling and crime. I would be startled to catch myself thinking in a remote way of my earlier self as another person.

Malcolm's rapid character change from satanic atheist to "religious fundamentalist" may seem surprising at first, but the roots of this potential transformation were laid down much earlier in Malcolm's life. The Nation of Islam was for Malcolm and his family a continuation in a different form of the script of Black pride combined with religiosity that they experienced in their home and family activities, before Malcolm's father was killed and the Garvey movement dissipated. It is important to note that Malcolm was the fifth member of his family to join the Nation of Islam and that it was his brothers and older sister who convinced him to take the teachings of Elijah Muhammad seriously. They had already found sustenance in Nation of Islam teachings that must have reminded them of their own early experiences. Like the Garvey movement and, indeed, influenced by it, the Nation of Islam taught Black pride and Black self-initiative. Followers of the Nation of Islam were taught to avoid all interactions with Whites, and told that Blacks could only succeed to the extent that they worked together for a common goal, which included returning to Africa. They both taught that economic independence was the key and that Black people needed to work together to acquire that independence. In addition, religious moral values were instilled both in the Nation of Islam and in Malcolm's family's home. Finally, it should be noted that Elijah Muhammad, who was already communicating with him in prison, would take a particular intimate interest in Malcolm, just as his father did, so that they developed a father-son relationship, one that would prove difficult for both of them as Malcolm outgrew the constraints of the Nation of Islam.

Roots of Conversion

I have compared the Nation of Islam and Malcolm's initial family situation at the level of scripts so that we have in the conversion of Malcolm, as with his other brothers and sister, a continuation of what might be called a commitment script, in which early positive socialization leads to the development of commitment to purposes in line with that socialization. But this commitment script is one that combines with a nuclear script, where good things turn bad, as the good original scene and script of Black pride and family affection was brought to an end by the death of Malcolm's father and the breaking up of their home and his mother's subsequent mental dissolution. The fact that most of Malcolm's family joined the Nation of Islam and were committed to its activities, with several brothers besides Malcolm becoming ministers, indicates a recovery of the original affective motivation and socialization that occurred in the Little family home. However, a key element that makes the Nation of Islam also tie in with the nuclear script is the role that the "White devil" plays in their mythology. For Malcolm, even before he understood anything else about the religion, this element made sense to him, and gave him an ingredient necessary to transform self-hate into another emotion—the hate of the White devil that he came to see as the source of the disintegration of his own family and of the lowly status in America of Black people. Malcolm would eventually overcome his nuclear script and undifferentiated hatred of White people, but it would be a struggle that would involve him in rejecting the Nation of Islam mythology and Black supremacist ideology and returning to the nonracist Garveyite view of Black nationalism as well as to converting to a nonracist form of Islamic religious ideology.

Robbing Black Identity

George Yancy

George Yancy is a professor of philosophy at Duquesne University and the author of Black Bodies, White Gazes *(2008).*

During his childhood Malcolm X was accepted by whites, but only as their black "mascot." To them, Malcolm's identity was nonexistence, and his core self remained invisible. Further, whites did not believe that Malcolm, because he was black, had capabilities of intelligence and sensitivity equal to their own. Such denial of black identity led to widespread black self-hatred, which Malcolm describes experiencing himself. Whites let blacks buy into their racist conviction: that to be black was to not be human.

At Mason Junior High School, Malcolm was the only Black student in the eighth grade. Although Malcolm mentions that he had not given thought to it before, he says that he disclosed to Mr. Ostrowski that he wanted to be a lawyer. Malcolm makes it clear that Ostrowski always provided encouragement to white students when asked for his advice regarding their future careers. Ostrowski replied:

> Malcolm, one of life's first needs is for us to be realistic. Don't misunderstand me, now. We all here like you, you know that. But you've got to be realistic about being a n-----. A Lawyer—that's no realistic goal for a n-----. You need to think about something that you *can* be. You're good with your hands—making things. Everybody admires your carpentry shop work. Why don't you plan on carpentry? People like you as a person—you'd get all kinds of work.

George Yancy, "Whiteness and the Return of the Black Body," *Journal of Speculative Philosophy*, vol. 19, 2005, pp. 230–233, 237. Copyright © 2005 by The Pennsylvania State University. Reproduced by permission of The Pennsylvania State University Press.

The Totalizing White Gaze

The reader will note the perverse construction of "We all here *like* you." Ostrowski is attempting to obfuscate the fact that he is a racist. He wants to clear his conscience by stating upfront his "affections" for Malcolm right before he violates Malcolm's body integrity, reducing him to a n-----, as someone who must learn to live with mediocrity and accept his place within the "natural" order of things. The young Malcolm is returned to himself qua [in the character of] n-----. "To forcibly strip someone of their self-image," as [law professor] Drucilla Cornell argues, "is a violation, not just an offense." Keep in mind that at this time Malcolm had already been elected class president and was receiving grades that were among the highest in the school. Yet, all that Ostrowski "saw" was a n-----. Despite the countervailing empirical evidence, Ostrowski "sees" more of whiteness's *same*. As Malcolm notes, "I was still not intelligent enough, in their eyes, to become whatever *I* wanted to be." Malcolm's point is consistent with what has been theorized thus far. First, within a white racist order of things, for the Black, there is apparently no being-as-possibility beyond the totalizing white gaze. As argued above, this is where perception, epistemology [the branch of philosophy that studies the nature of knowledge] and ontology [the study of the nature of being] are collapsed. Second, Malcolm's first-person perspective ("I desire," or "I have my own perspective on the world") is disrupted and rendered void vis-à-vis the third-person (white) perspective that has negatively overdetermined his Blackness.

Malcolm also describes his history teacher, Mr. Williams, as one who was fond of "n----- jokes." Of course, such "n----- jokes" were told at Malcolm's expense and no doubt "confirmed" many of the circulating myths consciously or unconsciously held by the white students. Malcolm notes:

> We came to the textbook section on Negro history. It was
> exactly one paragraph long. Mr. Williams laughed through it

Malcolm X speaks to a couple at a predominantly African American restaurant in the early 1960s. At this time, Malcolm only preached separation of blacks developing their own culture away from whites. Richard Saunders/Hulton Archive/Getty Images.

practically in a single breath, reading aloud how the Negroes had been slaves and then were freed, and how they were usually lazy and dumb and shiftless. He added, I remember, an anthropological footnote of his own, telling us between laughs how Negroes' feet were "so big that when they walk, they don't leave tracks, they leave a hole in the ground."

Although Malcolm *heard* these racist jokes, one might say, in keeping with Alexander G. Weheliye [in *Phonographies: Grooves in Sonic Afro-Modernity*], that "the white subject's vocal apparatus merely serves to repeat and solidify racial difference as it is inscribed in the field of vision." Whether through the ritualistic practice of Ostrowski putting Blacks in their "natural" place or through the racist jokes told by Mr. Williams, whites "adjusted their microtomes" [a microtome is an instrument used to cut tissue specimens into thin slices for examination under a microscope] and objectively cut away at Malcolm's reality. After such racist acts, Malcolm later admitted, "I just gave up." [French psychiatrist and revolutionary writer Frantz] Fanon [in *Black Skin, White Masks*] writes:

> I slip into corners, and my long antennae pick up the catch-phrases strewn over the surface of things—n----- underwear smells of n------—n----- teeth are white—n----- feet are big—the n-----'s barrel chest—I slip into corners, I remain silent, I strive for anonymity, for invisibility. Look, I will accept the lot, as long as no one notices me.

Black Mascot

Malcolm was reduced to the anonymous Black Other. He is returned to himself as an absence. Although "accepted" by whites, he is accepted only on their terms. [As Crispin Sartwell put it in *Act Like You Know: African-American Autobiography and White Identity*] "We [whites] will sweep you up into significance; we offer you a name: *our* name. But as we inscribe ourselves on you, we erase you." Hence, there is no genuine acceptance. There is only further distancing from the Black body. Only as a mascot does Malcolm come to experience his "acceptance" (his erasure!) by whites:

> They all liked my attitude, and it was out of their liking for me that I soon became accepted by them—as a mascot, I know now. They would talk about anything and everything with me standing right there hearing them, the same way people would talk freely in front of a pet canary. They would even talk about me, or about "n-----s," as though I wasn't there, as if I wouldn't understand what the word meant. A hundred times a day, they used the word "n-----."

Malcolm is cognizant of the hidden questions residing at the heart of white acceptance: How much are you (the Black) willing to erase of yourself? How much are you willing to conform to our (white) stereotype of you? How much can you hate yourself, while forgetting that it came from us? On this score, within the context of an anti-Black racist context, white acceptance comes at [a] price for Black people: a mode of nonbeing.

Inhuman Invisibility

Critiquing the "good-will" white, Malcolm notes, "I don't care how nice one is to you; the thing you must always remember is that almost never does he really see you as he sees himself, as he sees his own kind." Expounding upon the Ellisonian [based on Ralph Ellison's *Invisible Man*, which centers on the invisibility of blacks] theme of invisibility, Malcolm notes:

> What I am trying to say is that it just never dawned upon them that I could understand, that I wasn't a pet, but a human being. They didn't give me credit for having the same sensitivity, intellect, and understanding that they would have been ready and willing to recognize in a white boy in my position. But it has historically been the case with white people, in their regard for black people, that even though we might be *with* them, we weren't considered *of* them. Even though they appeared to have opened the door, it was still closed. Thus they never did really see *me*.

When one thinks about the long-range negative impact of Ostrowski's and Mr. Williams's racism on the young Malcolm, one can understand the dynamic of Black self-hatred. Self-surveillance or getting the Black body to regulate itself in the physical absence of the white gaze is a significant strategy of white racist ideology. Malcolm had internalized the white gaze. Through [his later] act of conking his hair, he policed his Black body in the image of whiteness:

> This was my first really big step toward self-degradation: when I endured all of that pain, literally burning my flesh to have it look like a white man's hair. I had joined that multitude of Negro men and women in America who are brainwashed into believing that the black people are "inferior"—

and white people "superior"—that they will even violate and mutilate their God-created bodies to try to look "pretty" by white standards.

. . . Within the white imaginary, to be Black means to be born an obstacle at the very core of one's being. To exist as Black is *not* "to stand out" facing an ontological horizon filled with future possibilities of being other than what one is. Rather, being Black negates the "ex" of existence. Being Black is reduced to facticity [the condition of being a fact]. For example, it is not as if it is only within the light of my freely chosen projects that things are *experienced* as obstacles, as [French philosopher Jean-Paul] Sartre might say; as Black, by definition, I am an obstacle. As Black, I am the very obstacle to my own meta-stability and trans-phenomenal being. As Black, I am not a project at all. Hence, within the framework of the white imaginary, to be Black and to be human are contradictory terms.

Malcolm X and the Black Bourgeoisie

Robin D.G. Kelley

Robin D.G. Kelley is a professor of American studies and ethnicity at the University of Southern California. His books include Inventing the Ghetto: Representing America's Urban Crisis *(2007) and* Freedom Dreams: The Black Radical Imagination *(2002).*

In his Autobiography *and in his speeches, Malcolm X railed against the "black bourgeoisie," those blacks who, in trying to fit into white culture, treated "lower-class" blacks with snobbery. But the same qualities Malcolm criticized in them—a strong work ethic, an emphasis on morality, and cleanliness in appearance—were shared by Malcolm and other members of the Nation of Islam. Because of this contradiction, the author of this viewpoint believes that Malcolm X had a love/hate relationship with the black bourgeoisie—although he concedes that hate was probably the stronger emotion.*

Unlike most black leaders prior to the early 1960s, including black working-class heroes such as A. Philip Randolph [a prominent twentieth-century civil rights leader] or Paul Robeson [often referred to as the perfect twentieth-century Renaissance man, he was a talented athlete, singer, author, and actor as well as a civil rights activist], Malcolm consistently identified with ordinary black working people and those displaced by the economy. He spoke their language and told their jokes. His was not simply another Horatio Alger [nineteenth-century author of many "rags-to-riches" stories; his name has become synonymous with the belief "if you

Robin D.G. Kelley, "House Negroes on the Loose: Malcolm X and the Black Bourgeoisie," *Callaloo*, vol. 21, Spring 1998, pp. 420–423. Copyright © 1998 The Johns Hopkins University Press. Reproduced by permission.

work hard, you will succeed."] story of how he rose out of poverty to become a hero. (And despite dozens of opportunities, he never sought wealth, leaving his family virtually penniless.) Rather, he invoked his experiences as an urban kid, former criminal, man of the streets, to show his audience that he knows where they are coming from and never forgot where he came from. In fact, he so depended on this identification with poor black folks—particularly the young—that he exaggerated his criminal exploits, his poverty, and his urban upbringing.

At the same time, Malcolm always had a love/hate relationship with the black bourgeoisie, though like most unconsummated relationships hate eventually became the dominant emotion. Even as a child in Lansing, Michigan, the sons and daughters of the black elite turned their noses up at the skinny red-head from that awful Little family. He was not only poor, but he was practically an orphan; his father was dead, and his mother had been committed to a mental institution. But he soon learned that these Negroes were nothing. He got his first real taste of black bourgeois pretentiousness when he moved to Boston with his half-sister Ella Little in 1941.

In the crazy, mixed-up world of intraracial class relations, World War II marked a critical moment. Of course, class conflict within African-American communities was hardly new. For some middle-class blacks, for example, the black poor had long been regarded as lazy, self-destructive, and prone to criminal behavior. On the other side of the class spectrum, as black sociologist Allison Davis found in his study of a small Mississippi town during the 1930s, "lower class" blacks often "accused upper-class persons (the 'big shots,' the 'Big Negroes') of snobbishness, color preference, extreme selfishness, disloyalty in caste leadership ('sellin' out to white folks'), and economic exploitation of their patients and customers." But during the 1940s, massive Southern black migration to Northern cities exacerbated cultural tensions between longtime urban residents and the newly arrived rural folk. African Americans born and raised in the North, particularly those who owned property and maintained a steady income, looked down on these newcomers and blamed them for neighborhood deterioration.

Snobbery and Millionaires' Airs

Ella owned a house on "the Hill," an elite section of the predominantly black Boston neighborhood of Roxbury. Her neighbors consisted of middle-brow black folks with high-brow pretensions, the most prominent of whom belonged to the so-called "Four Hundred." Massachusetts-born and -raised, the "Hill's" society Negroes fashioned themselves as colored equivalents of Boston Brahmins. They ridiculed Southern migrants and looked down on most working-class blacks despite the fact that some members of the "Four Hundred" were themselves service workers. Those who qualified for membership in the elite represented a wide range of occupations, from teachers, preachers, and nurses to Pullman porters, dining car waiters, and postal workers. From what Malcolm remembers, none were truly "bourgeois" in the classical sense; they did not own estates, factories, multi-million dollar firms, or exercise real power. What little power they enjoyed, as well as their self-proclaimed status, was dependent on white people. Malcolm often heard neighbors announcing, "'He's in banking,' or 'He's in securities.' It sounded as though they were discussing a Rockefeller or a Mellon—and not some gray-headed, dignity posturing bank janitor, or bond-house messenger."

Malcolm's peers were no better. When he first settled into Roxbury, they made fun of his clothes, which were a tad too small for him and obviously of bargain-basement quality. "To the teenage female sophisticates of the Hill," writes biographer Bruce Perry, "he looked as if he had just come from some farm." If that wasn't bad enough, Ella secured a job for him as a soda jerk at a neighborhood drugstore where his main clientele were the Hill kids. Serving them, he discovered, was even worse than dealing with them in various social settings. Although his employers were Jewish, in reality his immediate bosses were the black bourgeois patrons who came in by the droves and made incessant demands on him. It was steady work, but with it came all the ridicule and snobbery one could imagine. He vividly remembers having to endure these "penny-ante squares who came in there putting on their millionaires' airs."

Hill to Harlem to Prison

As he grew less and less tolerant of the Hill crowd, Malcolm began hanging out in the poorer sections of Roxbury where he "felt more relaxed among Negroes who were being their natural selves and not putting on airs." His newfound friend, Shorty, introduced him to the cool world of the zoot suit, the conk (straightened) hairstyle, and the lindy hoppers who spent their weekend nights at Boston's Roseland State Ballroom. When Malcolm donned his very first zoot suit, he realized immediately that the wild sky-blue outfit, the baggy punjab pants tapered to the ankles, the matching hat, gold watch chain, and monogrammed belt was more than a suit of clothes. It was a ticket into the "in crowd," a new identity that symbolized an increasingly militant and ultramasculine black street culture. The language and culture of the zoot suiters enabled Malcolm to reject white racism and patriotism, the rural folkways (for many, the "parent culture") that still survived in most black urban households, and the petit bourgeois attitudes of his "snooty" middle-class neighbors on the Hill. He found in the Roseland State Ballroom, and later in Harlem's Savoy, spaces of leisure and pleasure free of the bourgeois pretensions of "better class Negroes." For young Malcolm, his new world embodied the "true" black experience: "I couldn't wait for eight o'clock to get home to eat out of those soul-food pots of Ella's, then get dressed in my zoot and head for some of my friends' places in town, to lindy-hop and get high, or something, for relief from those Hill clowns."

Malcolm and his partners did not seem very "political" at the time, but they dodged the draft so as not to lose their lives over a "white man's war," and they avoided wage work whenever possible. His search for leisure and pleasure took him to Harlem where petty hustling, drug dealing, pimping, gambling, and exploiting women became his primary source of income. In 1946 his luck ran out; he was arrested for burglary and sentenced to ten years in prison.

Finding the NOI

His downward descent took a U-turn in prison when he began studying the teachings of the Lost-Found Nation of Islam (NOI), the black Muslim group founded by Wallace Fard and led by Elijah Muhammad (Elijah Poole). While he was no Horatio Alger, as I pointed out above, his rise from petty criminal to the NOI's leading spokesman contains all the classic elements of Horatio's story: he worked very hard, transformed himself, cleaned himself up, educated himself, began conducting himself in a respectable and dignified manner. Submitting to the discipline and guidance of the NOI, he became a voracious reader of the Koran and the Bible, and immersed himself in works of literature and history at the prison library. Behind prison walls he quickly emerged as a powerful orator and brilliant rhetorician. Upon his release in 1952, he was renamed Malcolm "X," symbolically repudiating the "white man's name."

As a devoted follower of Elijah Muhammad, Malcolm X rose quickly within the NOI ranks, serving as minister of Harlem's Temple No. 7 in 1954, and building up temples in Detroit and Philadelphia. Through national speaking engagements, television appearances, and by establishing *Muhammad Speaks*—the NOI's first nationally distributed newspaper—Malcolm X put the Nation of Islam on the map. But what impressed Malcolm more than high profile speaking engagements was grassroots organizing; he enjoyed "fishing" for converts in the bars and poolrooms where poor and displaced working-class men spent too much of their time.

Given Malcolm's experiences thus far, there could not have been a more appropriate movement than the Nation of Islam. Its leaders deliberately reached out to wayward youth and the "down and out," and they sustained a fairly antagonistic stance toward the rising black middle class. Indeed, as historian C. Eric Lincoln points out, most of NOI recruits "do not typically identify with the strivers of the black middle class. They tend to live comfortably, but frugally. The Movement continues to emphasize its affiliation with the working class." Although many converts discovered the Nation as prisoners, ex-hustlers, or jobless wanderers, the NOI's highly structured and disciplined environment instilled a strong work ethic into its congregation. Muhammad's followers worked, and worked very hard, but the majority lived in the ghettoes of North America and made barely enough to tithe [pay the zakat, a tax to support the needy and poor, as required of all Muslims]. . . .

Malcolm X's Quest for Racial Truth

Bashir M. El-Beshti

Bashir M. El-Beshti was professor of English literature at Wake Forest University in North Carolina before his death in 2005.

In this viewpoint Bashir M. El-Beshti traces how Malcolm X progressed toward racial truth with each transformation in his life. His first major step was his move to Boston, where he witnessed a completely different lifestyle for blacks than in Lansing. Boston gave him his first taste of racial pride. But although Malcolm stopped kowtowing to whites, he continued to try to live in their world, especially during his hustler days. This attempt at assimilation included, for instance, the conking (straightening) of his hair and his relationship with a white woman. In prison, his discovery of the Nation of Islam and its leader, Elijah Muhammad, taught him a form of black pride he had never known. And later, after his break with Muhammad and his trip to Mecca, Malcolm said that he had gained "a better understanding of America's entire racial dilemma," which led to greater racial truth.

By Malcolm's own account, the move to Boston which initiated his hustling career followed the infamous incident where Mr. Ostrowski, his English teacher, tells him "to be realistic about being a n-----," in response to Malcolm's unrehearsed desire of wanting to be a lawyer. "It was then," Malcolm writes, "that I began to change—inside." [In his *Autobiography*], the mature Malcolm praises Allah for the decision to leave Michigan and go to Boston, for "if I hadn't, I'd probably still be a brainwashed black Christian."

Bashir M. El-Beshti, "The Semiotics of Salvation: Malcolm X and the Autobiographical Self," *The Journal of Negro History*, vol. 82, Autumn 1997, pp. 363–367. Reproduced by permission.

The Search for Racial Pride

If this sounds like a strange expression of gratitude considering the nature of his Boston experience, it also renders that experience a necessary step towards avoiding the fate of a "brainwashed black Christian." In Boston, and more so in Harlem, Malcolm is submerged in the hustling underworld of the ghetto, an inverted world order where his brother Reginald has to pose as a thief in order to sell his goods. But Malcolm soon learns that one of the real natural places where he can be black is the underworld: the contradiction is that in order to become a natural black, he must become a hustler. Malcolm feels he belongs—the music, the dance are all symbolic of a natural rhythm, a medium of expressing a self long suppressed in Michigan. Malcolm's hustling energy, however, is cannibalistic as it feeds mostly on black victims. He paints a frightening picture of Darwinian world, "truly the survival of only the fittest."

The hustling underworld, nevertheless, afforded Malcolm a sense of community and racial pride: "Many times since, I have thought about it, and what it really meant. In one sense, we were huddled in there, bonded together in seeking security and warmth and comfort from one another, and we didn't know it." But while Malcolm the protagonist could feel the enormously liberating sense of a newly found identity, it would take the maturity of Malcolm, the autobiographer, to recognize the pathological, even absurd, nature of that identity: "How ridiculous I was! Stupid enough to stand there simply lost in admiration of my hair now looking white."

The conking of the hair, the white girlfriend, are signs of a psyche still dependent on the white ethic even as it ostensibly rebels against it. The syndrome is a familiar one: Malcolm recalls how his own father had favored him because "as anti-white as my father was, he was subconsciously so afflicted with the white man's brainwashing of Negroes that he inclined to favor the light ones, and I was his lightest child." In more clinical terms, Frantz Fanon has called this psychological phenomenon the "affective erethism," by which he means, "a constant effort to run away from his (the black man's) own individuality, to annihilate his own presence."

Hustler to Revolutionary

When Malcolm emerges from prison as the fiery Minister Malcolm X, proud of his blackness, confident of his superiority, conscious of his presence, the transformation seems complete. But as much as Malcolm would like for us to believe that his hustling days were over, that they belonged to an entirely different man, they still, nevertheless, form a large part of his working mentality. He knew, for instance, that he was being set up by the Nation of Islam after the announcement of his "silencing." "I hadn't hustled in the streets for years for nothing," he proudly proclaims.

But Malcolm was also proud of the fact that he could talk with the 'middle class' Negro and with the ghetto hustler just as easily as he could talk with the faculty and students at Harvard. His hustling experience is what separates Malcolm, by his own reckoning, from the so-called downtown black leaders; without it, he would probably be one of the downtown black leaders himself or, worse, "a brainwashed black Christian."

The transformation from hustler to revolutionary is not totally surprising or inexplicable:

> The hustler, out there in the ghetto jungles, has less respect for the white power structure than any other Negro in North America. The ghetto hustler is internally restrained by nothing. He has no religion, no concept of morality, no civic responsibility, no fear—nothing. To survive, he is out there constantly preying upon others, probing for any human weakness like a ferret.

Malcolm's hustling days, although recounted with disgust and self denunciation, taught him to break all bonds, to lose all respect for racist white society—the very condition necessary to preach the racially rigid ideology of the Nation of Islam.

But why would Malcolm be so susceptible to the teachings of a man who preached that he was the messenger of God and that the white man was the devil? The question is important for it raises the issue of sincerity and the charge of opportunism. The historic circumstances, Malcolm's own life and life's experiences made the assumptions easy and understandable, if not entirely believable. Elijah Muhammad simply brought these experiences home. "The very enormity of my previous life's guilt," Malcolm writes, "prepared me to accept the truth." Everything now seemed to be there for a reason:

> The teachings of Mr. Muhammad stressed how history had been "whitened"—when the white men had written history books, the black man simply had been left out. Mr. Muhammad couldn't have said anything that would have struck me harder. . . . This is why Mr. Muhammad's teachings spread so swiftly all over the United States, among all Negroes, whether or not they became followers of Mr. Muhammad. The teachings ring true—to every Negro.

For Malcolm, as David P. Demarest Jr. has pointed out, the myth of the genesis of man espoused by Elijah Muhammad is not necessarily true "but is presented rather as a useful metaphor, true in its expression of black superiority." From this perspective, Malcolm's experience with the Nation of Islam is an important step towards rehabilitating the self from the "psychological castration" inflicted upon it by white society. Malcolm, himself, characterizes the Nation as "having been a psychologically revitalizing movement." But it is a moral crisis again, this time instigated by Muhammad's sexual indiscretions, which leads to further metaphysical and psychological anxieties and undergirds the final phase in Malcolm's quest for identity.

Elijah Muhammad, founder and head of the Nation of Islam, delivers a speech in Chicago, Illinois on February 26, 1961, while Malcolm X applauds on the far left. Malcolm X was later shot and killed in 1965 by Nation of Islam members as a result of his separation from the organization. AP Images.

Actions vs. Values

"That which taketh away the reputation of wisdom in him that formeth a religion," [seventeenth-century English philosopher] Thomas Hobbes wrote in the *Leviathan* [his book on the formation of societies], "is the enjoining of a belief of contradictories." Elijah Muhammad did not practice what he preached; the Messenger of God who prescribed moral rectitude for his followers was himself a sinner. The revelation had a devastating effect on Malcolm:

> I felt as though something in nature had failed, like the sun, or the stars. It was that incredible a phenomenon to me—something too stupendous to conceive.

Elijah Muhammad had given Malcolm a sense of coherence and confidence, an awareness that one's endeavors and one's life make sense, that they are meaningful in the context in which life is lived. In other words, he had given him an identity. But identity also depends upon stable values and upon the conviction that one's actions and values are harmonious. In this respect, Elijah Muhammad had destroyed what he had given.

But the break with the Nation of Islam was inevitable from a moral as well as a political point of view. The perception of the Nation as "talk only" Muslims weighed heavily on Malcolm's soul. Here too, it pointed to the wide gulf between actions and values:

> If I harbored any personal disappointment whatsoever, it was that privately I was convinced that our Nation of Islam could be an even greater force in the American black man's overall struggle—if we engaged in more action.

Malcolm later conceived of an organization different from the Nation of Islam "in that it would embrace all faiths of black men, and it would carry into practice what the Nation of Islam had only preached." In a desperate effort to regroup, he quickly announced the establishment of Muslim Mosque, Inc. But the name itself and the announced charter implies an act of political compensation; while the attempt to "incorporate" anxiously marks Malcolm's political agenda as a separate entity from that of Muhammad's, it reduces Islam to merely a medium of political exchange. In Malcolm's mind, Elijah Muhammad had robbed the Islam of the Nation from any serious and meaningful political weight and spiritual significance. One can compensate for the political vacuity [emptiness] of the Nation; moral guidance and vision, on the other hand, cannot be incorporated. Then came the signs and the trip to Mecca.

New Vision: OAAU

Malcolm, of course, walks into the world of "orthodox" Islam in its purest, most idealistic form. The hajj as a ritual dissolves, if only temporarily, the divisions, the internal strife, the barriers separating humans; in other words, the reality of the Muslim world. It is a leveller matched only by death. The Izar and the Rida, the clothes worn during the state of Ihram [the state of holiness and purity a Muslim must enter in order to perform the hajj], however, eventually have to come off and when they do one can indeed tell a king from a peasant.

When Malcolm returns to his reality, it is not surprising that we find him struggling as to how to translate the ideal of "one god, one man" and the polyracial vision of the true Islam into a political program. "I'm man enough to tell you," Malcolm tells one reporter, "that I can't put my finger on exactly what my philosophy is now, but I'm flexible." Malcolm is not talking about his religious philosophy; submission to God had secured him in his dignity and saved him from fear and despair, from guilt and confusion. In Mecca, he was "blessed by Allah with a new insight into the true religion of Islam, and a better understanding of America's entire racial dilemma." Back in America, his newly formed Organization of Afro-American Unity [OAAU] and the ideology of Pan-Africanism are first attempts at a close political approximation of the moral vision of Islam. Malcolm of course was struck down by assassins' bullets while the OAAU was in its infancy; but it would be difficult to imagine that Malcolm would have remained static in the attempt to wed that vision to his basic mission of liberating the black man in America.

His Prophecy

In the conclusion of the autobiography proper Malcolm clearly places that mission, his life and death, within the prophetic mode:

> I know that societies often have killed the people who have helped to change those societies. And if I can die having brought any light, having exposed any meaningful truth that will help to destroy the racist cancer that is malignant in the body of America—then, all of the credit is due to Allah. Only the mistakes have been mine.

The turn on the conventional book dedication inevitably invites comparisons with the canceled original to Elijah Muhammad. In the original dedication Malcolm wrote:

> This book I dedicate to the Honorable Elijah Muhammad, who found me here in America in the muck and mire of the filthiest civilization and society on this earth, and pulled me out, cleaned me up, and stood me on my feet, and made me the man that I am today.

While the original emphasizes what Muhammad had done for him personally, stressing the conversion itself as the turning point in his life, the conclusion of the book, on the other hand, looks forward to his death at the hands of a society he tried to cure as a divine gesture, a sign of his prophecy.

Malcolm X Was Not a Racist

Rufus Burrow, Jr.

Rufus Burrow, Jr., is Indiana Professor of Christian Thought and professor of theological social ethics at Christian Theological Seminary in Indianapolis, Indiana. He is the author of five books, including God and Human Dignity: The Personalism, Theology, and Ethics of Martin Luther King, Jr. *(2006).*

The author of the following viewpoint believes that despite his numerous claims that whites were devils, Malcolm X was not a racist. Instead, Malcolm was merely responding to the lifetime of abuse that he, his family members, and fellow African-Americans suffered at the hands of whites. Malcolm's trip to Mecca in 1964 brought him in contact with whites who were not racist, instilling in him a sense that brotherhood could occur between people of all colors. But he understood that whites in America generally did not share the non-racist attitude of those he met in Mecca. Therefore, while he was more open to blacks and whites working together toward racial justice in America, he never became a total integrationist.

[Can it] accurately be said that Malcolm was at one time a racist; that through various experiences he was liberated from his racism; and that he ultimately became an integrationist, much like [Martin Luther] King and other "acceptable" civil rights leaders[?] Was Malcolm ever a racist, even when he thought he was?

On December 4, 1963 Elijah Muhammad, the self-avowed Messenger of Allah and leader of the Nation of Islam, silenced Malcolm for ninety days, ostensibly for the famous "chickens coming home to roost" statement made to a reporter follow-

Rufus Burrow, Jr., "Malcolm X Was a Racist: The Great Myth," *The Western Journal of Black Studies*, vol. 20, 1996, pp. 106–110. Reproduced by permission.

ing the assassination of President John F. Kennedy. On March 8, 1964 Malcolm announced that he was leaving the Nation of Islam and that he would be organizing a new movement. In the press conference he held a few days later he said that he would organize the Muslim Mosque, Inc., in which Blacks of all religious and non-religious persuasions could participate. This was followed by the announcement of the formation of a broader, more politically based organization, the Organization of Afro-American Unity (O.A.A.U.). This would be the political arm of his new organizational efforts, although had he lived longer he would likely have seen that he could not completely divorce politics even from his work through the newly established Muslim Mosque, Inc.

The Malcolm of the post-Mecca period said he would accept help from all quarters. Yet despite what he witnessed in Mecca and the softening of his view that the white man is the devil he was apprehensive about whites joining his organizations. He believed that sincere whites could do their best liberating work not by joining black organizations, but by organizing among themselves to fight the racism in their own communities and institutions. However, Malcolm conceded that he would consider allowing whites who were *John Brown types* [a reference to John Brown, a white man who was hanged in 1859 for attempting to start a slave rebellion] to join the O.A.A.U. But the truth, then and now, is that the history of white racism in this country and Malcolm's own experience of it caused him to never fully trust even the most radical whites. He therefore considered what Peter Goldman called "arm's-length alliances with the right kind of whites."

Although Malcolm left the Nation of Islam, he vowed that he would always be a Muslim. The pilgrimage to Mecca, in 1964, however, altered some of his earlier beliefs in Muhammad's version of the Islamic faith. Malcolm told of the effects of this new found truth upon his earlier belief that the white man is inherently racist.

Roots of Hatred

By the time he was thirteen Malcolm had already experienced enough to cause him to literally hate all white people for the rest of his life. And remember, hatred is not necessarily a bad thing. [African-American author] Alice Walker saw the positive value in hatred, pointing out that some people and institutions ought to be hated for the horrific crimes committed against persons and groups. Walker only insists that we "exercise our noblest impulses with our hate" and not allow it to destroy us.

At different periods Malcolm's father and three uncles were brutally murdered by white men. His family was broken up by the white state welfare authorities, who also had his mother institutionalized. The white people with whom he lived when placed in a detention center in Mason, Michigan treated him like a "mascot"—a pet or a non-person. In addition, his white eighth grade teacher told him that he had "to be realistic about being a n-----"—that he should give up the idea of being a lawyer and consider being a carpenter, since Blacks are so good with their hands. Malcolm was given this advice even though he was the class president and one of the brightest students in an otherwise all white school. At this point something left him. This was the first major turning point in his life, and no doubt had much to do with the way he would think about whites generally in ensuing years. By the time he was introduced to Elijah Muhammad's teachings on race he had already been primed by less than admirable experiences with whites.

Malcolm left school after the eighth grade, moved to Boston with his half-sister, Ella, and became fascinated with street life and just being in the presence of a critical mass of his own people. When he found himself in Harlem for the first time he was completely taken and knew this was where he wanted to be. He became a hustler, drug dealer and user, steerer of men to houses of sex pleasure, and a burglar.

When he and his best friend, Shorty, were caught, along with their white girlfriends in Boston, Malcolm was once again face to face with the meanness and racism of white men. According to Malcolm both his court appointed attorney and the judge were more concerned about his and Shorty's relationship with the two white women than the actual burglaries. The women were sentenced to one to five years, while Malcolm, at the age of twenty-one, was sentenced to ten. This was in 1946.

Anti-Christian, Not Anti-Religious

While in Massachusetts' Charlestown State Prison, Malcolm exhibited such a strong anti-religious sentiment that fellow inmates nicknamed him "Satan." But since the religion Malcolm knew best during this time was Christianity we may surmise that he had no use for this particular faith. Christianity was surely not the "true" religion for him because he believed it did not speak truly to the condition of Blacks. Indeed, it is not totally accurate to say that Malcolm had "anti-religious sentiments" during his imprisonment. Even the dreaded Satan has a religion! It is more accurate to say that the Malcolm of the early prison years was anti-Christianity, which is not the same as saying he possessed a strong anti-religious sentiment, and thus no religion at all.

Malcolm later converted to Islam after he was transferred to the Norfolk Prison Colony. He was introduced to the Islamic faith by his younger brother, Reginald. It was Reginald who first told him that Elijah Muhammad taught that "'the white man is the devil,'" and that there are no exceptions. When Malcolm thought back over his entire life and how he experienced whites, he was convinced of the truth of this claim. Furthermore, the white man is the cause not only of the predicament of Blacks in this country, but of racial-ethnic people the world over. Malcolm told Louis Lomax in 1963:

The white man is by nature a devil and must be destroyed. The black man will inherit the earth; he will resume control, taking back the position he held centuries ago when the white devil was crawling around the caves of Europe on his all fours. Before the white devil came into our lives we had a civilization, we had a culture, we were living in silks and satins. Then he put us in chains and placed us aboard the 'Good Ship Jesus,' and we have lived in hell ever since. (my emphasis)

Yet it is of interest to note that Malcolm often spoke of "the collective white man" as having "*acted like a devil.*" (my emphasis) This is quite different from the more metaphysical claim in the above quote that the white man *is* the devil. To be sure, Malcolm's reading of history while in prison confirmed the devilishness of white men throughout the world. But it did not substantiate the claim that the white man is by nature a devil.

Devilish Acts

Although I believe that Malcolm himself saw the sociological and historical truth in the claim that white men are devils, he was too smart to continue to give this metaphysical status. The truth is that sociologically, historically (and presently!) the white man has in fact acted like the devil on a massive scale all over the globe. None but a devilish person would do the things he has done (and does!). If Malcolm made a mistake at all it was to elevate to the level of metaphysics the claim that the white man is by nature a devil. All indicators are that as Malcolm matured he became increasingly uncomfortable with this stance. He knew that to say that white men are inherently devils implies that every single individual white person is a devil, a view that was clearly not substantiated by his later travels and his many conversations with white students, especially.

Malcolm could also see that the claim that the white man is the devil was inconsistent with the Islamic belief that there is one God who creates and sustains us all. For if the white man is truly by nature the devil, this would call into question the divine nature as well, since one God is presumably the creator of *all* persons. Later Malcolm tried to explain what was really intended by the statement that the white man is a devil.

> 'Unless we call one white man, by name, a 'devil,' we are not speaking of any *individual* white man. We are speaking of the *collective* white man's *historical* record. We are speaking of the collective white man's cruelties, and evils, and greeds, that have seen him *act* like a devil toward the non-white man. Any intelligent, honest, objective person cannot fail to realize that this white man's slave trade, and his subsequent devilish actions, are directly *responsible* for not only the *presence* of this black man in America, but also for the *condition* in which we find this black man here. You cannot find *one* black man, I do not care who he is, who has not been personally damaged in some way by the devilish acts of the collective white man!'

Malcolm's Audience

Although his attempt to explain and modify earlier views was not deemed newsworthy by those who control the media, whatever else the phrase "the white man is a devil" meant to Malcolm during the first dozen years he was in the Nation of Islam, it came increasingly to be little more than a rhetorical device to shock what moral sensitivities the white man may have possessed. However, as late as April 3, 1964 Malcolm was not at all certain that the white man even has a moral conscience. In addition, Malcolm linked the present condition of his people to the inhumanity of their theft from Afrika and their systematic forced enslavement in the Americas. Yet elsewhere he was adamant that this notwithstanding, Blacks alone can and must decide how to respond to the predicament forced upon them; that despite this they have within themselves the power of self-determination—the power to choose to move in new, liberating directions. Malcolm was always cognizant of the presence of moral agency in his people.

Malcolm said that it was in prison that he decided to devote the rest of his life to "telling the white man about himself...," and he wanted to do it to his face every chance he got. Right in prison he began to create opportunities during debates to expose the white man's devilish behavior in the world. But we must be careful not to conclude from this that such a stance itself either necessarily made Malcolm a racist, or that white America was Malcolm's primary audience. It was not! Despite his efforts to tell the white man the unequivocal truth about himself, Malcolm's most significant audience was, from beginning to end, his people. This, despite the fact that he loved being in front of the cameras of the white controlled media. He was less interested in teaching Blacks to hate whites, than teaching them to love and respect self, each other, their history and culture.

To be sure, there is no gainsaying the fact that even before Malcolm was released from prison in 1952 he believed the white man to be the devil and the cause of the socio-economic oppressive conditions of Blacks and other racial-ethnics. No one got more pleasure than Malcolm from addressing a crowd and—with large numbers of whites present—referring repeatedly and passionately to the white man as a "blond haired blue-eyed devil." Malcolm wrote the book on the art of overstatement, passionate and rhetorical speech, having learned as a child that he could usually get things done if he cried loudly enough. So he issued his diatribes against white racism and the economic exploitation of his people loudly and passionately.

Defining Racism

If one adheres to the classical social science definition of racism as the belief that one's own race is superior to another's by virtue of biological characteristics alone, it could be argued that the pre-Mecca Malcolm was a racist. But this definition, when applied to Blacks, is too narrow, as Malcolm himself held. He knew that the deleterious effects of racism on his people were not only a result of the ill-will of a few individual whites. Racism, for Malcolm, was not merely a presumption of superiority based solely on biological traits. Nor was it simply a psychological flaw, or a set of ideas that one has about another group. Rather, it is historic, systematized oppression that pervades every segment of this society—so much so that many whites are not even aware of their own racism! Racism is not only having ill-will toward a group on the basis of race, but having the socio-economic, political, and other forms of power to systematically act out this ill-will and to literally force one's will onto an entire race of people. When I talk about power here I do not mean what well meaning whites mean when they respond: "But isn't it true that everybody has power?" The type of power I am talking about gives one or their group the ability to literally and systematically force an individual and more particularly a group, to do things against their will. It is a type of power that enables a group to systematically carry out racist intentions without fear of legal, political, or economic retribution. It most assuredly is not true that everybody or every group has *this* type of power in the United States.

Although Malcolm did not have the peace of mind to articulate it this clearly in December 1964, he essentially held that the fact that Blacks were reacting militantly against white racism did not make them black racists. His classic illustration of this position was: "If you come to put a rope around my neck and I hang you for it, to me that's not racism." This response is that of a normal human being, not a racist. In Malcolm's view it is the abnormal human being who submits peacefully and willingly to lynching or to any act intended to dehumanize the person one is. For it is natural for human beings to defend themselves against physical attack. This in part is what it means to love and respect oneself.

Malcolm knew well the ominousness of racism. He described it as "the earth's most explosive and pernicious evil . . . , the inability of God's creature to live as One, especially in the Western world." No one, according to Malcolm, is as astute at playing the race game as the white man.

Considering Integration

Both before he went to Mecca and after his return, Malcolm spoke frequently of his willingness, indeed the need, to work with any group that was committed to helping Blacks to regain their dignity and sense of self-worth. The chief criterion for this stance was that there be a reasonable chance of securing meaningful, person-enhancing and community-developing results for the masses of black people, rather than for a select few among the black middle class and intelligentsia.

In a debate with [Black civil rights activist] James Farmer at Cornell University on March 7, 1962 Malcolm said that he would even consider going the integration route if he could be assured that the results would be "freedom, justice, equality, and human dignity" for his people. Yet for Malcolm the goal was not integration with white people. The goal was human dignity; the right to be fully human and all that that entails. Malcolm declared that what Blacks wanted was recognition and respect as persons, as human beings. Integrationism and separatism are only *means* to this end.

Even so, Malcolm's willingness to work with organizations committed to the enhancement of his people should not be taken to mean that he would submit uncritically to the methods of these groups and their leaders, nor that he would be an integrationist. Malcolm was his own man and did his own thinking, especially after the break with the Nation of Islam. In addition, as noted a moment ago he insisted that the criterion for his involvement with other groups was that there be clearcut possibilities for meaningful, substantive results for the masses of Afrikan Americans.

The Search for Truth

According to Malcolm it was in the holy city of Mecca that he witnessed a spirit and practice of brotherhood (regardless of color and nationality) that he had never experienced before. He reflected on this when he returned to the States.

> 'My trip to Mecca has opened my eyes. I no longer sub-scribe to racism. I have adjusted my thinking to the point where I believe that whites are human beings. . . .
>
> I'm *not* a racist. I'm not condemning whites for being whites, but for their deeds. I condemn what whites collectively have done to our people collectively.'

As late as January 18, 1965 (approximately one month be-fore he was murdered) Malcolm insisted that he was not only *not* a racist, and was against racism and discrimination in any form, but that he simply believed in human beings, and that every person "should be respected as such," regardless of their color. Indeed, what Malcolm relished most about the experi-ence in Mecca was "'The *brotherhood*! The people of all races, colors, from all over the world coming together as *one*! It has proved to me the power of the One God.'"

[African-American poet] Maya Angelou reflected on this change in Malcolm, and how much more deeply she came to appreciate him for his courage to make this change because of his deep love for truth. She had always respected and appreci-ated Malcolm,

> 'but my appreciation increased really noticeably after he said, "I have always said whites were blue-eyed devils, but I have been to Mecca and I have seen whites with blue eyes with whom I felt a brotherhood, and so I can no longer say this—that all whites are evil." It took a lot of courage to say

that—an amazing amount of courage. It took an incredible amount of insight, first, to give up what one had said for years and years and say, "Just wait a minute, let me relook at this, let me rethink, respeak this," but he had the courage to do so and the insight to do so, and then the courage to say so, which just humbled me. He had no loyalty to misconceptions. He was intelligent and courageous enough to admit when a position no longer held true, and that's amazing. Very few people have that; most people would rather like to say what they say they believe in and then repeat themselves instead of saying, "I'm not in love with the position, I'm in love with the search for truth"—and that was Malcolm.'

American Whites the Problem

Malcolm was not naive about his changed perspective regarding race (a change, it might be added, that began to take shape even *before* he went to Mecca!). He was quite aware that the experience of brotherhood in Mecca was one thing, but the lived-experience of Blacks in the United States was altogether different. "'When I got back into this American society,' he said, 'I'm in a society that might preach [brotherhood] on Sunday, but they don't practice it on *no* day.'" Blacks in America were not treated as he had been treated in Mecca, and upon his return he did not pretend differently. Malcolm was not interested in trying to force brotherhood upon whites who did not want it.

However, Malcolm did conclude that "whiteness" or the term the "white man" had more to do with an attitude, a way of thinking, or with the white man's actions toward Blacks. It had less to do with skin color alone. White complexioned men in Mecca had been the most brotherly he had ever met. But this was no indication of a similar situation in the States. The brotherliness of American whites would have to be tested by the extent of their treatment of Blacks on a day to day basis. "The *problem* here in America," said Malcolm, "is that we meet such a small minority of individual so-called 'good,' or 'brotherly' white people."

After Mecca, Malcolm was not sentimental regarding racism in this country. Although he was desperately trying to turn the corner on this issue—a corner that both his earlier "Black Muslim" image and the media converged to obstruct—he was still as angry after as before the pilgrimage to Mecca regarding the effects of racism on his people. Despite his rejection of the earlier view that the white man is innately evil and a devil, Malcolm would not let the American white man off the hook so easily. White American society is deeply entrenched in racism, and would not likely extricate itself in his or his childrens' lifetime. The truth that Malcolm learned in Mecca caused him to turn up the heat on the race issue when he returned to the States. Therefore he was not less, but more critical of the American white man.

Yet Malcolm could still say that his friends now included representatives from nearly every group imaginable.

> 'I have friends who are called Capitalists, Socialists, and Communists! Some of my friends are moderates, conservatives, extremists—some are even Uncle Toms! My friends today are black, brown, red, yellow, and *white*.

Achieving Self-Love

The Malcolm of the post-Mecca period said that he was not a racist, and that he did not "subscribe to any of the tenets of racism." Indeed, in the *Autobiography* we find him saying (after Mecca) that the white man is not inherently evil. He not only denied being a racist, but went further, claiming: "*I've never been a racist.*" (my emphasis)

Malcolm conceded that Elijah Muhammad's version of Islam was not the true form, especially regarding race. True Islam requires that one be one hundred percent "against racism." It also requires that persons be judged not by physical attributes, but by their behavior and deeds. Malcolm was not against people whose skin happened to be white. He was against both what whiteness had come to symbolize in the world, viz., the oppression of people of color, and "against those who practice racism." The test for judging persons is what they do and what they practice. But this did not diminish his belief that the white man will continue to be the enemy of the black community until he rids himself of his racist institutions. In addition, and significantly, Malcolm made it clear that his first concern is the wellbeing of his own people.

Few have written more wisely and perceptively than [African-American novelist and essayist] James Baldwin as to whether Malcolm X was a racist.

> Malcolm was not a racist, not even when he thought he was. His intelligence was more complex than that: furthermore, if he had been a racist, not many in this racist country would have considered him dangerous. He would have sounded familiar and even comforting, his familiar rage confirming the reality of white power and sensuously inflaming a bizarre species of guilty eroticism without which, I am beginning to believe, most white Americans of the more or less liberal persuasion cannot draw a single breath. *What made him unfamiliar and dangerous was not his hatred for white people but his love for blacks, his apprehension of the horror of the black condition, and the reasons for it, and his determination so to work on their hearts and minds that they would be enabled to see their condition and change it themselves.* (my emphasis)

Malcolm loved his people; loved things Afrikan and Afrikan American. His aim was to teach his people to love and respect themselves and each other. He knew what they could accomplish through love of self, their black heritage, and through unity. It was this possibility which produced more fear and concern in the white man, not the idea of teaching Blacks to

hate whites. Malcolm knew that black liberation and empowerment would come only when his people learned to love
themselves.

The Transformation of Malcolm X

Nancy Clasby

Nancy Clasby is a senior lecturer in the department of English at the University of Miami in Coral Gables, Florida.

In this viewpoint, published nine years after Malcolm X's death, Nancy Clasby asserts that Malcolm X's spiritual transformation embodied a new consciousness that was emerging among non-whites throughout the world. After his 1964 trip to Mecca, Malcolm X no longer thought that all whites were the enemy of blacks. In Mecca he felt true oneness with others, black and white. This experience liberated him from white thought patterns, and he was finally able to fully claim his identity as a black man. Still, this transformation did not change Malcolm's overall opinion of American whites, who, he thought, had a long way to go toward liberation. Nor did it lessen the anticipation of violence in his life. But now Malcolm was reborn, with hopes that eventually a new brotherhood could be formed in the United States.

[Malcom X experienced many transformations of self during his life.] Malcolm's final metamorphosis occurred during his trip to Mecca and his immersion in the ferment of the African struggle for independence. Because the structures of Elijah Muhammed's movement were simply reverse models of the old structures, and did not, in practice, reflect the creative energy of liberated men, the old patterns of jealousy, competition and the urge to control were bound to emerge. The many prohibitions sprang from an artificially

Nancy Clasby, "The Autobiography of Malcolm X: A Mythic Paradigm," *Journal of Black Studies*, vol. 5, September 1974, pp. 27–33. © 1974 Sage Publications, Inc. Republished with permission of Sage Publications, Inc., conveyed through Copyright Clearance Center, Inc.

conceived notion of discipline, rather than from the necessities of successful resistance and were certain to be broken. The Manichean [dualistic philosophy] design of good versus evil was simple and useful for a time, but it was not, in the long run, "true." [According to French psychiatrist and philosopher Frantz Fanon] the truth in a situation of struggle is "that which promotes the emergence of the nation: it is all that protects the natives," and destroys the "living lie" of the colonial situation.

The "truth" was occurring outside the Muslim movement in the streets. By 1962–1963, the demonstrations and sit-ins had become mass movements. Elijah Muhammed kept the Muslims separate, and Malcolm grew increasingly restive.

> I thought privately that we should have amended, or relaxed, our general non-engagement policy. I felt that where black people committed themselves, in the Little Rocks and Birminghams and other places, militantly disciplined Muslims should also be there. . . . It could be heard increasingly in the Negro community: "Those Muslims *talk* tough, but they never do anything, unless somebody bothers Muslims."

Elijah Muhammed's movement could not envision liberation, but only coexistence with the old structures—escape, along a parallel track.

Oneness and Liberation

Malcolm astonished the world in April 1964 by his letter from Mecca asserting "the Oneness of Man."

> We were *truly* all the same (brothers)—because their belief in one God had removed the "white" from their *minds*, the "white" from their behavior and the "white" from their attitude.

The dramatic change in attitude toward whites was symptomatic of a profound transformation in which he shook off the pattern of "white" thought structures and assumed his final identity as a black man: El Hajj Malik el Shabazz. The old Muslim pattern, while breaking with the concept of the "white master," has retained the power patterns which presume some sort of master. The Muslims were in the situation of the "liberi," or sons, in the primitive society described by Norman O. Jones. In this society, the sons of the father were distinguished from his slaves by the title, "liberi," which signified that they "owned themselves." The genuinely liberated man is the one for whom the very concept of being "owned" is unthinkable. The father-owner and the self-owner, with its implicit connotation of a divided self, must disappear before liberation is possible. Previously Malcolm had attempted to bend the power-flow to accommodate himself and his people—to substitute a more likeable owner—but at this point he transcended the western power structure altogether. "Mankind's history has proved from one era to another that the true criterion of leadership is spiritual. Men are attracted by spirit. By power, men are forced. Love is engendered by spirit. By power, anxieties are created."

Fanon's analysis of the third-world revolutionaries describes the same emerging insight as the primitive Manicheism adopted at the beginning of the struggle.

> Racial feeling, as opposed to racial prejudice, and that determination to fight for one's life which characterizes the native's reply to oppression are obviously good enough reasons for joining in the fight. But you do not carry on a war, nor suffer brutal and widespread repression, nor look on while all other members of your family are wiped out in order to make racialism or hatred triumph. Racialism and hatred and resentment—"a legitimate desire for revenge"—cannot sustain a war of liberation.

Pinpointing the Enemy

The reason for this is the dawning recognition that some Blacks are "whiter than the Whites," that some profiteer and exploit the struggle, and that the system meant to replace op-

Malcolm sits and meets with Prince (later King) Faisal al-Saud during his pilgrimage to Mecca in 1964. Malcolm's trip to Mecca transformed him, leading him to fully claim his identity as a black man and to preach integration instead of separation. Pictorial Parade/ Hulton Archive/Getty Images.

pression is itself "yet another system of exploitation." As the natives look around them in the course of the struggle, they also notice that the monolithic [massive] façade of the white populace is crumbling. Some whites do not join in the hysteria, others condemn the repression. "The scandal explodes when the prototypes of this division of the species go over to the enemy, become Negroes or Arabs, and accept suffering, torture and death." Such a confusing turn of events will either thwart the revolutionary struggle, or metamorphose it into a quest for a totally new and organic society. Fanon says that "in the end, everything depends on the education" of the people. "Political education means opening their minds, awakening them, allowing the birth of their intelligence; as [French poet and author Aimé] Cesaire said, it is 'to invent souls.'"

Malcolm's trip to Mecca brought him to the awareness that the enemy was an international power arrangement which grew out of a certain thought pattern: "It's the American political, economic and social *atmosphere* that automatically nourishes a racist psychology in the white man." This alteration in view did not result in an unqualified acceptance of white allies, since the fact remained that American whites are, whether they wish to be or not, products of social patterns which make an organic or "spiritual" awareness very unlikely.

Nor did Malcolm's change of view suggest a lessened expectation of violent struggle. Violence remained endemic to the situation and affected all of its creatures. His detachment had given way to what [political philosopher] Hannah Arendt calls "compassion"—a fierce, radical goodness which "shares the elementary violence inherent in all strength." Such passion sweeps away the old forms and engenders new souls. In the political sphere, compassion addressed to changing conditions in order to ease human suffering "will shun the drawn out wearisome processes of persuasion, negotiation and compromise which are the processes of law and politics, and lend its voice to the suffering itself, which must claim for swift and direct action, that is, for action with the means of violence." Malcolm foresaw that violence would inevitably touch him: "It's a time for martyrs now. And if I'm to be one, it will be for the case of brotherhood. That's the only thing that can save this country. I've learned it the hard way—but I've learned it."

Malcolm Reborn

The personal consequences of Malcolm's change were profound. For the first time in his life he "stood before the Creator of All and felt like a complete human being." Cut off from his past, alone in a throng of identically dressed pilgrims of all races, he stood in the airport at Jedda and he had "never felt more alone and helpless, since (he) was a baby." Malcolm, reborn, was quickly and completely taken into the human family by the Orthodox Muslims. "Love, humility and true brotherhood was almost a physical feeling wherever I turned. . . . All ate as One, and slept as One. Everything about the pilgrimage atmosphere accented the Oneness of Man under One God." He made himself vulnerable to others, and they sustained him. The others were "physically present for him . . . liberated from categories." This special gift of unity lasted during his pilgrimage through a newly liberated Africa. Everywhere he went the African people embraced him and wept and cheered.

> I reflected many, many times to myself upon how the American Negro has been entirely brainwashed from ever seeing . . . himself as a part of the non-white peoples of the world. The American Negro has no conception of the hundreds of millions of other non-whites' concern for him: he has no conception of their feeling of brotherhood for and with him.

A New Brotherhood

The Nigerians named him Omowale, "the son who has come home." Patricia Robinson's article ["Malcolm X, Our Revolutionary Son and Brother"] speaks of him in the broadest sense as the son who rejects his role as imitator and successor of the great father and returns instead, "to us, the women, the girl children, the poor and the have-nots, who are still ruled in dumb suffering." For [South African poet and political activist] W. Keorapetse Kgositsile, "Malcolm was our sun, our son," who taught his people to love. "Words of love become acts of love recreating the powerful gods in us. . . . Malcolm underwent the internal revolution and internalized the Black Revolution, the world revolution."

He returned to America determined to forge a new brotherhood like that he had experienced in emerging Africa:

> 'Life is lived at an impossibly high temperature. There is a permanent outpouring in all the villages of spectacular gen-

erosity, of disarming kindness and willingness, which cannot ever be doubted, to die for the "cause." All this is evocative of a confraternity, a church, and a mystical body of belief at one and the same time.'

Malcolm went back into the ghetto to form the Organization of Afro-American Unity, a revolutionary brotherhood and a new model for a human and spiritual society. His ideal was pastoral, in the sense of the revolutionary described by [the scholar] A.M. Elmessiri who may not believe that the world of simplicity and spiritual purity "actually exists, yet believes in the possibility of vision and its superiority over fact and reality."

Malcolm's "Turning About"

The machinelike efficiency of the old Malcolm was gone, lost along with "the sickness and madness of those days"; his "nerves where shot, his brain tired." He seemed to falter in conducting the business of the new organization, often ignoring his lieutenants and falling more into the company of the numberless, nameless people who sought him out on the streets, in restaurants, wherever he went. He drew closer to his family, telling Sister Betty, "We'll all be together. I want my family with me. . . . I'll never leave you so long again." Though his forces appeared to be scattered, his influence was increasing, unseen and unrecognized, because of the powerful meaning of his change.

[Civil rights leader and author] Eldridge Cleaver's testimony as to the meaning Malcolm's development held for him reveals the effects on many desperate men.

> We had watched Malcolm X as he sought frantically to re-orient himself and establish a new platform. It was like watching a master do a dance with death on a highstrung tightrope. He pirouetted, twirled, turned somersaults in the air—but he landed firmly on his feet and was off and running.

After the assassination, he wrote, "I have, so to speak, washed my hands in the blood of the martyr, Malcolm X, whose retreat from the precipice of madness created new room for others to turn about in." Because Malcolm X had "turned about," many others were able to accomplish the difficult maneuver of coming to birth.

"A Living and Splendid Death"

He sought to educate by embodying the new myth, he "invented souls" by drawing others into participation in the emerging black identity. Malcolm's efforts to pass on what he had experienced sprang from his hunger to "fill men's minds and feast their eyes with human things, and create a prospect that is human because conscious and sovereign men dwell therein". Such a dream could not survive in America in 1965. Malcolm was about to go from history into myth, and he knew it. "Anyone who wants to follow me and my movement has got to be ready to go to jail, to the hospital, and to the cemetery before he can be truly free."

His life ended on the stage of the Audubon Ballroom in a hail of assassin's bullets. But his significance was just beginning as the American incarnation of the desperate men who are plucking a new humanity from the global whirlwind of violence. It was, in Aime Cesaire's words, a "living and splendid death."

Autobiography of Malcolm X: Myth or Truth?

Peter Dailey

Peter Dailey is a New York attorney and writer.

The influence of Malcolm X's Autobiography on black writers, students, and activists has been incredible. It revolutionized thinking about race, politics, and the status quo. But Bruce Perry's 1991 book about Malcolm X, Malcolm, The Life of a Man Who Changed Black America, *questions whether the Autobiography tells more myth than truth. Perry conducted more than 400 interviews with family and friends of Malcolm and reported that their accounts often contradicted the Autobiography. In this viewpoint Peter Dailey points out that, regardless of such discrepancies, it is undeniable that Malcolm's life story, like that of many other black men and women of his time, was very much shaped by racism. Dailey argues that, even if specific details of the Autobiography are exaggerated or even made up, Malcolm X will still remain an influential figure in society.*

For a generation of black writers, students, and activists, reading the *Autobiography [of Malcolm X]* was a transforming experience. For [African-American author] bell hooks it "revolutionized my thinking about race and politics"; for [black writer] Thulani Davis it "opened my mind, moved it away from provincial, frightened thinking." People as varied as [author and civil rights leader] Eldridge Cleaver and [the second African-American Supreme Court Justice] Clarence Thomas described it as a decisive influence.

[German philosopher Friedrich Wilhelm] Nietzsche argued that after death men are understood worse than men of

Peter Dailey, "Who Was Malcolm X?" *Dissent Magazine*, vol. 40, Summer 1993, pp. 348–350. Copyright © 1993 by Dissent Publishing Corporation. Reproduced by permission.

the moment, but *heard* better. With the resurgence of interest in Malcolm, his speeches and writings received the sort of respectful attention they had never had before. "By any means necessary!" and other slogans extolling black pride and assertiveness took on an emblematic clarity. Attempts by scholars to reconstruct a coherent philosophy from his hundreds of speeches, however, were largely unsuccessful; his words were often contradictory, reflecting the expectations of his audiences, which were as varied as the Socialist Workers party, the Harvard Law School, and street-corner meetings on 125th Street.

One writer has described his speeches as a "loosely strung set of positions that were changing even as he announced them." Malcolm himself acknowledged to a reporter that "I'm man enough to tell you that I can't put my finger on exactly what my philosophy is now." Paradoxically, these very ambiguities ultimately enhanced his influence. [African-American scholar] C. Eric Lincoln noted that the "projections of what he was about to do range from a seat on the board of the Urban League to a [Fidel] Castro-type armed revolution."

Autobiography: Truth or Myth?

That [Alex] Haley's account was at variance with the more pedestrian actuality of Malcolm's life has long been suspected by literary scholars. . . . The full extent of the omissions and distortions that gave it shape was not known, however, until the publication in 1991 of Bruce Perry's *Malcolm, The Life of a Man Who Changed Black America*. Although marred by reductive psychoanalyzing and deficient in other respects, Perry's book represented an impressive piece of research. Malcolm was only thirty-nine when he was murdered, and was survived by his wife, mother and numerous siblings, friends, and associates who had witnessed the events described in the *Autobiography*. In all Perry interviewed over four hundred people, conducting, in addition, a similarly exhaustive search of police, prison, court, and F.B.I. records. In the twenty-five years since Malcolm's apotheosis these sources had gone largely unconsulted, a curious circumstance given the intensity of interest about him.

The book that resulted contains a number of revelations. One of the framing devices of the *Autobiography* is a series of dramatic confrontations with racism. Malcolm relates how his parents were driven from their home in Nebraska by hooded night riders; persecution follows them and when Malcolm is an adolescent, their house near Lansing, Michigan, is burned down by the Black Legion, a KKK-type organization. The book states that Malcolm's Garveyite [follower of the teachings of the black nationalist Marcus Garvey, who preached that black Americans should return to Africa] father was ultimately murdered by whites, who threw his body on the streetcar tracks to make his death appear accidental. In addition, he accounts for what he apparently felt was the incongruity of advocating black pride while possessing a light skin color by explaining that his West Indian grandmother had been raped by a white man. Perry convincingly demonstrates that these events either did not occur or were fundamentally misrepresented.

Malcolm's descriptions of his life in the Roxbury and Harlem ghettos are similarly exaggerated. The teenaged Malcolm of the *Autobiography* is a young lion, subjugating anyone and everything to his will, but saved ultimately from a life of degradation by his prison conversion to the Nation of Islam. Like much else in the book, this is a romance. The poverty he experienced was a good deal more demoralizing and the remedies to which he resorted more desperate than his account would indicate. What is indisputable is that his early life in a depression-era welfare family was profoundly shaped by racism. Nor was the process by which he remade himself any less remarkable. The story, however, of how this was accomplished would have required someone with considerably more self-knowledge than Malcolm to tell it.

Malcolm's "Change of Heart"

David Bradley correctly notes that we are left with "a subtly altered figure—more intriguing, more intelligent, certainly more human." Especially provocative is the disclosure that as a young man one of the expedients to which Malcolm turned was homosexual prostitution. Unfortunately, Bradley acknowledges, as the facts are more generally known, subtlety is likely to be the first casualty.

Although these discoveries have been widely publicized, less remarked upon are those concerning Malcolm's central epiphany during the Hajj to Mecca, which Perry scrutinized skeptically, ultimately casting considerable doubt on its genuineness. In 1959 Malcolm had traveled extensively in the Middle East and experienced many of the same things he later claimed struck him with the force of revelation. Noting the methodical way Malcolm undertook to publicize this change of heart, writing scores of postcards to newsmen, and giving his puzzled subordinates elaborate instructions about how he wanted the press handled, Perry argues convincingly that his pilgrimage provided the pretext for abandoning a racial ideology that for some time had been politically burdensome.

True Feelings Toward Whites

His private feelings about whites were undoubtedly more complicated than his rhetoric as a minister for the Nation would suggest. Accounts that treat Malcolm as a product of the northern ghetto ignore the extent to which his early life in largely rural communities had been intertwined with the lives of white people. Although this experience could not have been other than deeply embittering, his white schoolmates had been sufficiently aware of the young Malcolm's exceptional qualities to elect him class president, and he apparently had

had an affectionate relationship with a white foster family. This familiarity may explain the comparative equanimity with which, even during his days as a Muslim firebrand, his personal dealings with the white devil were conducted.

Of more significance than his private racial beliefs is the extent to which he had succeeded in renouncing racist political appeals. [Writer] Peter Goldman believed that at his death Malcolm was as convinced as ever that all white people were the enemies of all black people. David Bradley argues that "he did not give up hating or his accusations of racism. He simply learned to hate institutions."

It would be wrong, of course, to describe such beliefs as racist, although when translated into street-corner oratory, the distinction can seem elusive. Nevertheless, a number of troubling episodes are difficult to reconcile with the larger and more humane vision his admirers later ascribed to him. Particularly disturbing were statements he made just weeks after his return from Mecca that appear to countenance an attack by a gang of black teenagers during the course of a robbery of a white-owned Harlem clothing store, in which the shopkeeper's wife was stabbed. [Black civil rights activist] James Farmer, who asked Malcolm why his new outlook was not reflected in the speeches he gave every Saturday at Harlem Square, was told: "Brother James, you must be enough of a politician to understand that if a leader makes a sudden right angle turn, he turns alone." About the only thing that can be said with any degree of certainty is that, as [Tom] Kahn and [Bayard] Rustin noted, "his hostility to whites was becoming less absolute."

The Cult of Malcolm

Does the truth about Malcolm in fact matter? For those to whom Malcolm is less a historical figure than a mythic presence, it has become irrelevant. Ron Simmons, in an interview in *Malcolm X: In Our Own Image* argues that "many a people nave been united and have grown strong on premises that were basically a lie." A less sanguine [African-American film-maker] Marlon Riggs notes however that "at some point the lie becomes disabling." This phenomenon is hardly unprecedented. To answer the needs of the present, a figure out of the shared past is transformed into a moral exemplar—with varying degrees of violence to the historical record. The cult surrounding Malcolm reflects the failures in our time of black nationalism, and a consequent yearning, Adolph Reed argues, "for a different reality in lieu of engaging the one that actually confronts us." If the cases of John F. Kennedy, Robert E. Lee, and Abraham Lincoln are any indication, in time, the connection becomes so remote, the memory of failure or sense of loss so attenuated, that for a new generation the exemplar no longer has a meaning and is returned to history. For Malcolm X this is unlikely to happen anytime soon.

Social Issues
in Literature

CHAPTER 3

Contemporary
Perspective on Racism

The Impact of 9/11 on Arab and Muslim Americans

Shibley Telhami

Shibley Telhami is Anwar Sadat Professor for Peace and Development at the University of Maryland, a nonresident senior fellow at the Saban Center for Middle East Policy at the Brookings Institution, and a former adviser for the U.S. Mission to the United Nations and the Iraq Study Group.

After the terrorist attacks on September 11, 2001, Muslim Americans and Arab Americans were placed in a difficult situation. First, they had to reflect on their identity: were they Muslims and Arabs living in America or Americans with Muslim and Arab ethnicities? Also, as was expected, these groups were subjected to increased discrimination and racial profiling. But while fears of Middle Eastern peoples increased after the attack, a year later polls revealed that most Americans had a positive view of the Muslim religion. As for the post-9/11 Arab-American perspective, they overwhelmingly agree that the United States' primary focus should be on resolving the Palestinian-Israeli dispute.

In a *New York Times* article appearing a week after the horror befell America on September 11, a Muslim woman [presented] her dilemma this way: "I am so used to thinking [of] myself as a New Yorker that it took me a few days to begin to see myself as a stranger might: a Muslim woman, an outsider, perhaps an enemy of the city. Before last week, I had thought of myself as a lawyer, a feminist, a wife, a sister, a friend, a woman on the street. Now I begin to see myself as a brown woman who bears a vague resemblance to the images of terrorists we see on television and in the newspapers. I can only

Shibley Telhami, "Arab and Muslim America: A Snapshot," *Brookings Review*, vol. 20, Winter 2002, pp. 14–15. Copyright © 2002 Brookings Institution. Reproduced by permission.

imagine how much more difficult it is for men who look like Mohamed Atta or Osama bin Laden."

Excruciating moments like those the nation experienced [in] September [2001] test the identity of all Americans, but especially those whose identity may be caught in the middle. Many Arab and Muslim Americans lost loved ones and friends in the attacks in New York and Washington, and others had loved ones dispatched to Afghanistan as American soldiers to punish those who perpetrated the horror (Muslims are the largest minority religion in the U.S. armed forces). But many also had double fears for their own children. On the one hand, they shared the fears of all Americans about the new risks of terror; on the other, they were gripped by the haunting fear of their children being humiliated in school for who they are.

Two Partially Overlapping Communities

There is much that's misunderstood about Arabs and Muslims in America. Although the two communities share a great deal, they differ significantly in their make-up. Most Arabs in America are not Muslim, and most Muslims are not Arabs. Most Arab Americans came from Lebanon and Syria, in several waves of immigration beginning at the outset of the 20th century. Most Muslim Americans are African American or from South Asia. Many of the early Arab immigrants assimilated well in American society. Arab-American organizations are fond of highlighting prominent Americans of at least partial Arab descent: Ralph Nader, George Mitchell, John Sununu, Donna Shalala, Spencer Abraham, Bobby Rahal, Doug Flutie, Jacques Nasser, Paul Anka, Frank Zappa, Paula Abdul, among many others. Like other ethnic groups in America, Arabs and Muslims have produced many successful Americans whose ethnic background is merely an afterthought.

Arab Americans now [as of 2002] number more than 3 million, Muslims roughly 6 million (though estimates range from 3 million to 10 million). The income of Arab Americans is among the highest of any American ethnic group—second only to that of Jewish Americans. Arab Americans have become increasingly politicized over the years. According to a recent survey, proportionately more Arab Americans contribute to presidential candidates than any other ethnic group—and the groups surveyed included Asian Americans, Italian Americans, African Americans, Hispanic Americans, and Jewish Americans. Over the past decade especially, Arab-American political clout has increased. Although Arab Americans were long shunned by political candidates, President Clinton became the first sitting president to speak at conferences of Arab-American organizations, and both President Clinton and President Bush have normalized ongoing consultations with Arab- and Muslim-American leaders. In the fall 2000 election, presidential candidates sought the support of Arab Americans, not only for campaign contributions, but also as swing voters in key states, especially Michigan. The September 11 tragedy, coming just as Arab-American political clout was ascendant, has provided a real test for the community's role in American society and politics.

Impact of September 11

For Arab and Muslim leaders, the terrorist crisis has been like no other. It has forced them to contemplate profoundly their identity. Are they Arabs and Muslims living in America, or are they Americans with Arab and Muslim background? The answer came within hours after the terrorist attacks. Major Arab and Muslim organizations issued statements strongly condemning the attacks, refusing to allow their typical frustrations with issues of American policy in the Middle East to become linked to their rejection of the terror. Rarely have Arab and Muslim organizations in the United States been so assertive.

The enormity of the horror, the Middle Eastern background of the terrorists, and the terrorists' attempt to use religion to justify their acts have inevitably led to episodes of discrimination against Arabs and Muslims, as well as against those, such as Sikhs, who resemble them. But the support that both Arabs and Muslims received from thousands of people and organizations far outweighed the negative reaction. Arab and Muslim organizations were flooded with letters and calls of empathy from leaders and ordinary Americans, including many Jewish Americans, for most understood that at stake were the civil liberties of all Americans.

Public Reaction

In large part, the public reaction was a product of quick decisions and statements by President Bush and members of his cabinet, members of Congress from both parties, and local political leaders. The president in particular acted quickly to make two central points that seem to have resonated with most of the public. The first was that the terrorists did not represent Islam and that Osama bin Laden must not be allowed to turn his terror into a conflict between Islam and the West. The second was that Muslim and Arab Americans are loyal Americans whose rights must be respected. Bush's early appearance at a Washington, D.C., mosque with Muslim-American leaders underlined the message.

The message seems to have gotten through. Despite the fears that many Americans now associate with people of Middle-Eastern background, a survey conducted in late October by Zogby International found that most Americans view the Muslim religion positively and that the vast majority of Arabs and Muslims approve the president's handling of the crisis. (Among Arab Americans, 83 percent give President Bush a positive performance rating.) Moreover, 69 percent of Arab Americans support "an all-out war against countries which harbor or aid terrorists."

Sura Hassan, a nineteen-year-old student, lives in the Detroit suburb of Dearborn, which is arguably the capital of "Arab America" with an estimated 300,000 Arab Americans in southeastern Michigan. After the attacks of September 11th, discrimination and racial profiling of Arab Americans increased dramatically. AP Images.

Arab-American Response

Certainly, the events of September 11 will intensify the debate within the Arab and Muslim communities in America about who they are and what their priorities should be. One thing is already clear. Although both communities have asserted their American identity as never before and although 65 percent of Arab Americans feel embarrassed because the attacks were apparently committed by people from Arab countries, their pride in their heritage has not diminished. The October survey found that 88 percent of Arab Americans are extremely proud of their heritage. So far, however, the terrorist attacks have not affected the priorities of the Arab public in America as might be expected, given Arab Americans' deep fear of discrimination.

Typically, Arab-American organizations highlight such domestic issues as secret evidence and racial profiling and such foreign policy issues as Jerusalem, Iraq, and the Palestinian-

Israeli conflict. While Arab Americans, like other minorities, are involved in all American issues and are divided as Democrats and Republicans, as groups they inevitably focus on issues about which they tend to agree. The situation is no different from that of American Jews, who are also diverse, but whose organizations largely focus on issues of common interest.

Given the fear of profiling that Arab Americans had even before September, one would expect this issue to have become central for most of them since September 11. And for many it certainly has. Arab-American organizations, especially, have focused on it. But the findings of the Zogby poll among Arab Americans in October were surprising. Although 32 percent of Arab Americans reported having personally experienced discrimination in the past because of their ethnicity, and although 37 percent said they or their family members had experienced discrimination since September 11, 36 percent nevertheless supported profiling of Arab Americans, while 58 percent did not. Surprisingly, 54 percent of Arab Americans believed that law enforcement officials are justified in engaging in extra questioning and inspections of people with Middle Eastern accents or features.

Searching for Solutions

Though their views on profiling have been mixed since September 11, Arab Americans have been considerably more unanimous on one subject—the need to resolve the Palestinian-Israeli dispute. Seventy-eight percent of those surveyed agreed that "a U.S. commitment to settle the Israeli-Palestinian dispute would help the president's efforts in the war against terrorism." Although most Arab Americans are Christian and mostly from Lebanon and Syria—and only a minority are Palestinians—their collective consciousness has been affected by the Palestinian issue in the same way that Arab consciousness in the Middle East has been affected. In a survey I commissioned in five Arab states (Lebanon, Syria, United Arab Emirates, Saudi Arabia, and Egypt) last spring, majorities in each country consistently ranked the Palestinian issue as "the single most important issue to them personally." The role of this issue in the collective consciousness of many Arabs and Muslims worldwide is akin to the role that Israel has come to play in contemporary Jewish identity.

Like all Americans since September 11, Arab and Muslim Americans are searching for solutions to terrorism. Like all Americans, they are also finding new meaning in aspects of their identity to which they might have given little thought a few short months ago.

Muslim Americans Carry a Double Burden

Marilyn Elias

Marilyn Elias writes primarily about medical and science issues for USA Today.

Since the terrorist attacks of September 11, 2001, many Muslim Americans have been harassed and discriminated against, during a time when they themselves have been worrying about the threat of terrorism. This double burden, of worrying about terrorism and being blamed for it, in addition to the harassment and discrimination, has led to mental health difficulties for some. Since the attacks, the American Psychology Association and many individual therapists have seen a rise in stress, anxiety, and depression in Muslim Americans. Those who have been least vulnerable to these difficulties are those that have a strong sense of group identity and a support group of non-Muslims.

Motaz Elshafi, 28, a software engineer, casually opened an internal e-mail at work last month. The message began. "Dear Terrorist."

The note from a co-worker was sent to Muslims working at Cisco Systems in Research Triangle Park, N.C., a few days after train bombings in India that killed 207. The e-mail warned that such violent acts wouldn't intimidate people, but only make them stronger.

"I was furious," says Elshafi, who is New Jersey-born and bred. "What did I have to do with this violence?"

Reports of such harassment and discrimination against Muslims are rising, advocacy groups say. A USA TODAY/

Gallup Poll of 1,007 Americans shows strong anti-Muslim feeling. And the hard feelings are damaging the mental health of U.S. Muslims, suggest new studies to be released at the American Psychological Association meeting starting Thursday in New Orleans.

Thirty-nine percent of respondents to the USA TODAY/ Gallup Poll said they felt at least some prejudice against Muslims. The same percentage favored requiring Muslims, including U.S. citizens, to carry a special ID "as a means of preventing terrorist attacks in the United States." About one-third said U.S. Muslims were sympathetic to al-Qaeda, and 22% said they wouldn't want Muslims as neighbors.

Verbal harassment and discrimination correlate with worse mental health in studies of Muslims and Arab-Americans since 9/11, says psychologist Mona Amer of Yale University School of Medicine.

In her new study of 611 adults, thought to be the largest ever done on Arab-Americans, they had much worse mental health than Americans overall. About half had symptoms of clinical depression, compared with 20% in an average U.S. group, Amer says.

Muslims, who made up 70% of the study's participants, had poorer mental health than Christians. Those less likely to be depressed or anxious were people who kept their ethnic or religious ties but also had relationships with other people in the community. And more Christians than Muslims lived this "integrated" lifestyle, Amer says.

Though Muslims said they wanted more contact with Americans of other religions, it may be easier for Arab Christians to integrate, Amer speculates.

"They share the mainstream religion. Muslims may have different kinds of names or dress differently and, especially since 9/11, they're ostracized more."

Bias Leads to Depression

Virtually no mental health research was done on U.S. Muslims before 9/11, so her findings can't be compared with earlier studies. A new publication, the *Journal of Muslim Mental Health*, began publication in May, signaling concern about the growing problems and lack of research.

Many therapists are counseling more Arab-Americans and Muslims since 9/11, Amer says. Also, in surveys of Muslim spiritual leaders [that were] reported at the psychological association meeting, the imams report a surge in worshipers seeking help for anxiety and stress related to possible discrimination.

Reports of such abuses skyrocketed in the first six months after 9/11, fell in 2002 and have climbed again since the Iraq war began in 2003, according to data kept by the Council on American-Islamic Relations, an education and advocacy group in Washington, D.C.

The number of assault and other discriminatory complaints filed with the group jumped from 1,019 in 2003 to 1,972 in 2005, says Arsalan Iftikhar, national legal director.

Nobody knows what proportion of U.S. Muslims encounter discrimination; even Muslims disagree.

"I don't think there's a Muslim out there who hasn't felt some kind of fallout from 9/11," says Jafar Siddiqui, 55, a real estate agent in Lynnwood, Wash. "I myself have been invited to 'go home' at least once a month." Siddiqui has been a U.S. citizen for 20 years.

Despite an increase in harassment since 9/11, "many, many have not felt any discrimination," says Farid Senzai, research director of the Detroit-based Institute for Social Policy and Understanding, a non-profit started four years ago to do research on Muslims.

Harassment charges claiming unreasonable arrest and detention have garnered the most publicity. But discriminatory acts in everyday life—in shops, schools and at work—are reported about as frequently to the American-Islamic relations council.

Elshafi, who got the nasty e-mail at work, still wonders at the boldness of a person who would send such a note. The sender was asked to apologize to several employees who filed complaints with Cisco's human resources department, says Elshafi, who didn't file a complaint.

"We wouldn't confirm a specific internal incident on the record," says Cisco's Robyn Jenkins Blum, who adds, "It is Cisco's policy not to tolerate artificial divisions or harassment of any individual."

Elshafi, a worshiper at the local mosque, says he has received a lot of support from non-Muslim friends at work. "After 9/11, people would say, 'Don't worry, 'Taz, we've got your back.'" He says Muslims are not doing enough to educate people about their religious practices. "We need to talk about our beliefs, know our neighbors."

People such as Elshafi are least vulnerable to becoming depressed due to bigotry, says John Dovidio, a University of Connecticut psychologist and expert on prejudice. "He gets strength from his group identity and support from the outside."

Many are not nearly as fortunate. Children of recent immigrants, women who wear the traditional head scarves or long robes and Iraqi-Americans often aren't faring as well, according to reports at the psychological association meeting.

In Seattle, Hate Free Zone Washington, an education and advocacy group, was launched five years ago to oppose backlash against local Muslims, Sikhs (sometimes mistaken for Muslims) and Arab-Americans. "We've seen an increase in bias-based harassment since 9/11," says Amelia Derr, the group's education director.

Derr says she has seen some Muslim children so traumatized by violent bigotry that she wonders whether they'll ever recover. Last October, a Seattle high school junior who had faced verbal harassment was assaulted in gym class. He suffered a hemorrhage behind his eye and a collapsed lung, Derr says. "The good thing is that the student who did it was convicted of a hate crime."

But the beaten boy won't go back to school, she says. "He's terrified. You can see how damaged he has been. He won't look you in the eye; he just shrinks back. He won't talk." The family came from Afghanistan four years ago, she says.

Even some who were born and raised in the USA feel their religious freedom has limits. Jafumba Asad, 32, of Tulsa stopped wearing the traditional dark robe after 9/11. "It's bad enough just wearing a head scarf. I get nasty stares every day. Wearing full cover makes it harder to get a job. It scares people," says Asad, a community college teacher and graduate student.

Muslim women who wear head scarves are more likely than those who don't to say they face discrimination and a hostile environment, according to a study [that was] presented at the psychological association's meeting by Alyssa Rippy of the University of Tulsa. The scarves make Muslim women stand out and could change behavior toward them, she suggests.

A few years ago, in a Wal-Mart parking lot, Asad says two men approached her and aggressively shouted "Y'all ought to be (expletive) locked up!" Pregnant at the time, she quickly backed away and then realized there were parked cars behind her. "I felt trapped and very vulnerable. I'm pregnant. I didn't know if they were going to get violent." Luckily, she says, they just walked away.

The mother of three girls says she developed ulcers a few months after 9/11. "I feel stressed a lot."

In Rippy's study, Muslim men were just as likely as women to report discrimination but more likely to become mistrustful and wary because of it. That can encourage sticking with your own group, "which intensifies feelings of paranoia," she says.

Iraq War's Fallout

Men may back away more than women because they feel discrimination could have more serious consequences for them, for example being pegged as a terrorist or jailed, Rippy says.

The USA TODAY/Gallup Poll suggests Americans have greater fear of Muslim men than women: 31% said they'd feel more nervous flying if a Muslim man was on the plane; 18% said they'd be more nervous with a Muslim woman. The poll, conducted July 28–30, has a margin of error of plus or minus 3 percentage points.

The Iraq war has made its mark on U.S. Muslims as well, psychologist Ibrahim Kira will say at the meeting. In his study of Iraqi-Americans, the more time people spent listening to the radio and watching TV news about the war, the more likely they were to have post-traumatic stress disorder. Many of them had relatives still in Iraq, and stress-disorder rates were high: 14% compared with 4% for the U.S. population, Kira says.

Tuning in to war news also correlated with more stress-related health problems, such as high blood pressure, headaches and stomach trouble, Kira says.

Although the war creates special problems for Iraqi-Americans, they also share a key challenge with other Muslims: lack of trust from people living here. Many Americans clearly don't trust those of the Muslim faith. In fact, 54% said they couldn't vote for a Muslim for president in a June *Los Angeles Times*/Bloomberg poll. That compares with 21% who turned thumbs-down on an evangelical Christian and 15% who wouldn't cast their ballot for a Jew.

Amer believes the world has changed for U.S. Muslims since Sept. 11 but says: "I don't think Americans understand what's happened. Muslims have the same anxieties and anguish about terrorism as everyone else in the U.S. At the same time, they're being blamed for it. They're carrying a double burden."

Students of All Races Need Effective Discipline

Joshua Frank

Joshua Frank is vice principal of Pierce School in Brookline, Massachusetts.

Out of fear of being labeled a racist, and guilt for the "privilege" of their skin color, white educators often avoid disciplining black students. As a result, black students do not receive the feedback they require to excel in school. The author acknowledges that while white privilege does exist, it is not a privilege that was asked for. He also points out that students of all ethnicities often try to avoid responsibility for their poor choices. So if some are not held accountable by their teachers, they will not have the opportunity to improve. If teachers establish classroom limits, keep confrontations private, use nonjudgmental language, and set realistic goals, all involved—teacher, student, and parent—will benefit.

Educators often talk about the need for relevant and representative curriculum for students of color, the need to recruit more educators of color, and the reality of white privilege. At my school, we hold "courageous conversations" among staff and a diverse group of families to nurture a dialogue that breaks through the boundaries of race.

We rarely discuss, though, concerns involved in white educators disciplining students of color. I find myself wondering how often white educators lose opportunities to fully communicate with black students and their parents because we fear that feedback and criticism will be viewed as racist.

I view this as a very important concern because when discipline works, by holding students accountable in a way that

Joshua Frank, "Effective Discipline Across Racial Lines," *The Education Digest*, vol. 73, September 2007, pp. 62–64. Reproduced by permission.

they feel is fair and aimed at helping them, instead of resisting or shutting down they are less likely to misbehave again and more likely to make academic progress.

As a white educator, I'm aware that each student's race is an important part of his or her identity.

When I work with a student of color, I'm aware that our being of different races will play a role, almost always unspoken, in our interaction. I have also recently been encouraged to think of my whiteness as a racial identity that proffers privilege rather than something that serves as the unacknowledged norm against which others are measured.

My whiteness bears some scrutiny and analysis as it affects my ability to work with students of color, particularly in the area of discipline where issues of fairness and privilege often come into play. Students of all races try to deflect responsibility for their misbehavior.

Resist Blame

But in interactions between white educators and students of color, the students also often try to express dissatisfaction with a sense of color blindness and white privilege that feels unfair. After almost 20 years of work in diverse public schools, I have concluded that the best way to become accountable for one's privilege is to resist blaming oneself for it.

It is best to move beyond the guilt, fear, and anger that often result from the mix of privilege and good intentions that white educators bring to their work with students of color and to learn to work more effectively across racial boundaries. These feelings are often hidden unconsciously behind genuine good intentions, and sometimes evolve into a sense of powerlessness to "help" that then turns into anger.

While white privilege exists, it is unearned, because none of us chooses the color of our skin. Yet any thoughtful person who enjoys an unearned privilege will experience some guilt. As a result, white educators often try to convince students of color and their families that they want to "help" them achieve at the same level as the white majority.

If that "help" fails to result in high achievement and positive behavior, guilt can easily give way to fear related to being branded a racist. Yet there seems to be a powerful taboo against acknowledging these feelings.

Setting Goals

Nobody likes to feel guilty or afraid. Most public educators genuinely want to help others. But I believe that many white educators get tired of feeling guilty and afraid, and, most of all, they begin to feel powerless. Some respond by getting angry, often in ways of which they are unaware.

The dynamic evolves from "I want to use my white privilege to help" to "What if they call me a racist?" to "What if I am becoming a racist?" to "What if they find out I've become a racist?" and finally to "I tried to help, but it didn't work, so it must be their fault."

So how can white educators address color-blind thinking and the reality of white privilege and work effectively with students of color? My suggestions rest on a few simple ideas:

- When educators focus on goals for students as individuals, based on measurement of long-term improvement, they may simultaneously acknowledge race and transcend some of its barriers.
- Students' progress should be measured against their own past performance and within a long time frame. Educators should avoid a deficit model and instead build on strengths.
- Feedback to students and families should be balanced between positive and negative, be specific, and be presented with a view to the long-term future.

When educators help students set goals, the interaction is student centered. Consider the difference between saying, "I

First year teacher Greg Butler gives special attention to second grader James Lee at Hawthorne Elementary School in Indiana. Approximately 95% of teachers are white in Indiana, while the students come from a diverse range of backgrounds. AP Images.

don't want you to disrupt my classroom," and saying, "I want you to earn a 1 or 2 for behavior, but today was a 4. Can you make tomorrow a 1 or 2?" Also, in this example, the goals suggest an ongoing relationship that has a future.

When the student doesn't meet expectations, then the discussion is about what happens tomorrow, as much as what went wrong today. In measuring progress toward long-term goals, students may be able to quickly experience some success and leave behind a sense of unfairness.

In setting goals, educators should first set baselines. Avoid comparisons with other students and mention of past failures or misbehavior. Then share with students and their families specific feedback on progress toward long-term goals.

Confront in Private

If a student doesn't respond to limits during class, confront the misbehavior calmly and, when possible, privately. Avoid code words like "disrespect" or "attitude," which may cut off, rather than nurture, a positive working relationship.

Describe behavior in a non-judgmental tone. Specificity communicates fairness and objectivity, helps set clear goals for students, and helps parents work in tandem with the school. Parents are in a much stronger position when they can say, for example, "Do your homework and keep your hat off in the classroom," instead of "You've got to do better and stop having an attitude."

The potential payoff for students and educators alike to taking a constructive approach to academic functioning and discipline is great. Educators, students, and parents who communicate with each other comfortably and see themselves as working together in a spirit of fairness and shared concern for the students will most likely succeed.

Black Students Still Lag Behind in Student Achievement

Carol M. Swain

Carol M. Swain is a professor of political science and law at Vanderbilt University and the founding director of the Veritas Institute, both in Nashville, Tennessee. Her book Black Faces, Black Interest: The Representation of African Americans in Congress *was published in 1994.*

Blacks from both the lower and middle class are trailing behind whites and Asians in educational achievement. In this viewpoint, Carol M. Swain argues that affirmative action impedes central middle-class black achievement, because it misinforms black students about educational expectations and lowers their sense of ability. Lower-class black children, on the other hand, have greater obstacles to overcome: for instance, they often come from families lacking in education, they are more likely to be affected by alcoholism and abuse, and they often need to start working jobs to support themselves and their families. Swain says that poverty can destroy the self-esteem of these students. But, she continues, having just one adult saying "you're smart" and "you can achieve great things" can make all the difference for children in this situation.

> The lower economic people are not holding up their end of the deal. These people are not parenting. They are buying things for their kids—$500 sneakers for what? And won't spend $200 for "Hooked on Phonics." ... People marched and were hit in the face with rocks to get an education, and now we've got knuckleheads walking around.
>
> —*Bill Cosby*

Carol M. Swain, "An Inside Look at Education and Poverty," *Academic Questions*, Spring 2006, pp. 47–52. Copyright © 2006. Reproduced with kind permission from Springer Science and Business Media and the author.

Comedian Bill Cosby's remarks presented on the anniversary of the 1954 *Brown v. Board of Education* desegregation case [which overturned laws that established separate schools for blacks and whites] were directed at a subgroup of the black population who were not present to hear his remarks. His remarks, however, are just as applicable to the lifestyle choices of more affluent blacks, whose children are also often failing to reach their potential for reasons that cannot easily be dismissed as racism. Like the lower-classes, too many of the middle-class suffer higher than normal rates of dysfunction when it comes to incarceration rates, crime, drug abuse, illegitimacy, and other social ills. My concern here is with educational achievement and competitiveness. Unfortunately, not enough blacks at any socioeconomic level are faring as well as they should. The black middle-class is treading water and missing the mark.

There is a well-documented black/white achievement gap in educational performance that affects every economic level. Black children reared in families earning $50,000 a year score no better than whites and Asians reared in families earning from $10,000 to $20,000 per year. These stark differences in achievement levels manifest themselves during the K-12 years. Tests sponsored by the National Assessment of Education Progress (NAEP) show a familiar pattern of blacks lagging behind other groups. Studies have shown that by senior year, the average black high school student functions at a skill level four years behind the skill levels of white and Asian students. This pattern occurs even in top school districts where blacks lag behind and often complain about having difficulty understanding their assignments. Something other than white racism and sub par schools must be contributing to black underachievement.

Mixed Blessings of Racial Preferences

A part of the problem must lie in parental expectations and societal messages that reinforce the negative stereotypes that blacks are less capable and less likely to benefit much from the application of higher standards imposed by teachers and institutions. It is too often the case that well-intentioned teachers and counselors reinforce black students' affirmations that they are not able to make it academically, and when difficulties do arise, the parents are quick to blame teachers and the educational system rather than properly attributing lapses to what is not being said and done at home.

This essay speaks to issues involving middle-class and lower-class African Americans. I cast my lot with those observers who see cultural norms and lowered expectations as being partially responsible for the fact that blacks lag behind other racial and ethnic groups in academic achievement. In some cases, I believe that the situation has been worsened by the existence of certain forms of affirmative action that have not made distinctions among minorities of different socioeconomic classes. Indeed, for decades, society has signaled to blacks that it is okay for them to be less competitive than other groups. I believe this has had a harmful impact on the aspirations and self-confidence of many blacks who have internalized these very wrong negative messages.

Relevant to this discussion is my non-traditional background as a high-school dropout who, despite the odds, earned a Ph.D. and tenure from two elite universities. . . . I have had more than 20 years of exposure to the problem about which I now write. Time in the trenches as a student and a professor informs this discussion. I focus on the black underachievement gap because of its persistence, because of my kinship with African Americans, and because of my deeply held beliefs that racial preferences have been a mixed blessing for our nation.

A Serious Look at Affirmative Action

Let me support my position with some observations. As an older undergraduate student in the 1980s, I often encountered other black college students struggling with grade point averages at or below a 2.00 on a 4.00 scale who voiced aspirations of wanting to become lawyers and doctors. If I challenged them directly by responding, "But I thought you needed a 3.0 to get into law or medical school"—almost invariably the student would respond, "Oh, they have to let us in. They have to let us in, because of affirmative action." Now, I don't believe that many of those students were actually admitted to professional schools, but the misinformation led some genuinely to believe that traditionally white professional schools were obligated to take them, regardless of their less-than-stellar performance. This perception, I believe, affected how hard these students trained. The knowledge of affirmative action's double standards no doubt caused some to neglect burning of the midnight oil.

Could such attitudes affect the level of exertion that a person puts forth towards the achievement of goals and aspirations? Could such beliefs be a factor in the well-documented fact that black students in college *underperform* their SAT scores—that is, black students with the same SAT scores as whites exhibit a considerably lower performance in college than white students. Racism and the difficulty of adjusting to the social environment are common explanations for the discrepancy.

Affirmative action has affected students in other ways as well. I have often encountered black students who seemed immobilized by the belief that "we" were incapable of competing effectively with whites. Some had internalized white racist notions of black inferiority. I came away from many conversations fully convinced that the people with whom I was talking did not have a clue as to how hard successful people often work to attain their goals. In an effort to draw the knowledge gleaned from my roots as a high school dropout and one of 12 children raised in rural southern poverty, I have pulled together some ideas of what I think can be done to address as-

University of Missouri-Kansas City freshman Destiny Byers watches as a first-grader learns to count at the Santa Fe Accelerated Elementary School in Kansas City, Missouri. Byers is part of UMKC's Institute for Urban Education program that teaches inner city students to become inner city teachers. A lot of minority students from lower-class families are not encouraged to devote themselves to educational pursuits, and having one positive adult influence can make a huge difference. AP Images.

pects of the current black/white achievement gap at the secondary level, where it all starts. It is my hope that with concerted efforts we can nip some of the problems in the bud. Perhaps, in a few years, the felt need for racial preferences in higher education will increasingly fade as more and more minorities become competitive in all areas of life.

Addressing the Problems of Middle-Class Blacks

Perhaps the easiest problem to address is the situation where middle-class black students are not achieving as much as they should, given their resources. Here the choices may be a matter of values. Parents have the resources to become aggressively involved in the education of their children. One of the easier things that parents can do is to be aware of the content of curriculum and the level of difficulty of the courses chosen by students and guidance counselors. One study explaining the black/white test gap showed that black students who took the SAT had not followed the same academic track as white students. The white test-takers were far more likely to have completed courses in geometry and higher-level mathematics such as trigonometry and calculus. Black students took fewer literature and honors writing courses. They were also less likely to invest in such test-coaching courses as Kaplan and the Princeton Review: known to raise scores by 100 points or more. Clearly, these are areas where a more pro-active stance can yield greater positive outcomes.

Middle-class parents can hire private tutors, they can restrict the amount of time their children watch television and play sports, they can monitor peer-group associations, and they can make sure that their offspring take full advantage of all enrichment opportunities offered by schools and other institutions. A dramatic increase in the number of black parents willing to push their children as though affirmative action programs never existed and no longer do would result in positive achievement outcomes.

The Very Different Situation of Lower-Class and Underclass Blacks

"They're standing on the corner and they can't speak English. I can't even talk the way these people talk: 'Why you ain't.' 'Where you is.' And I blamed the kid until I heard the mother talk. And then I heard the father talk. . . . Everybody knows it is important to speak English except these knuckleheads. You can't be a doctor with that kind of crap coming out of your mouth," spouted Bill Cosby. Indeed, sympathies are with the lower-class blacks that were not in the room with Cosby. Until I was a student at the community college where I earned my first degree, I used the vernacular black English of my parents. "He don't," and "she don't" rolled effortlessly off my tongue, because that was how we talked at home. Fortunately, I was eventually corrected by one of my black classmates in a most gentle manner. "Oh," she said, "I think you meant to say that she doesn't have a car." That was enough to correct that particular grammatical problem for me, but others persisted, such as subject/verb disagreements that still occasionally crop up.

My parents were uneducated. My father had a third-grade education, my mother, an intelligent woman, dropped out in the tenth grade, and my stepfather had no apparent education at all. None of my siblings—seven brothers and four sisters—ever graduated from high school. Although I too dropped out of school after completing the eighth grade, by the grace of God I managed to earn five college and university degrees from an array of institutions. I was by no means the smartest of the 12—I was just the one who escaped.

Ignorance is rampant among the poor. Before I dropped out of school, I believed that my situation was hopeless and that only rich people could go to college. For a number of reasons, I dropped out of school and married at 16 years of age. Affirmative action and scholarships were totally outside of my sphere of knowledge. For families like mine, affirmative action might as well not have existed. When I did enter college, such need-based programs as Pell Grants, federal loans, and work study enabled me to move to the next stage where race and merit worked together to create opportunities for poor minorities who defied the stereotypes.

Better Choices for Poor Students

Talented students from disadvantaged families like mine are dependent on the goodwill of adults outside the family who can give them hope and steer them toward programs and courses that can be of assistance to them and their families. Students whose parents will not take full advantage of available options and resources should not be penalized by rules and requirements that often limit opportunities in the best programs to students whose parents are actively involved in the school. Few of the children of the truly poor will have parents able and willing to work in the schools and participate in parent/teacher conferences. Why not let willing adult mentors fill the gap by serving informally as surrogate parents when it comes to certain types of involvement? Even the most disinterested parents would probably welcome the input from a concerned volunteer.

It is also important to steer some students into alternative educational programs. We must accept the fact that not all smart students are college bound. There are students who have no interest in college. Many struggle to master basic reading, writing, and math skills. Some students should be steered toward appropriate vocational programs or community colleges that offer remedial education, vocational training, and opportunities to transfer credits to four-year colleges and universities. What is needed are new focused and concerted efforts linking teachers, guidance counselors, and concerned adults to identify and encourage students to stay in school, work hard, and avail themselves of resources to improve their life chances. How many potential leaders, scientists, and university professors are trapped in poor schools and desperate family situations?

Many factors affect the performance of students from poor families. In my family we missed school because we lacked proper clothes for the weather and because we did not have alternative transportation to school if we missed the bus. I can remember times in which I attended school without deodorant or sanitary napkins. What most people take for granted is often not available to the poor. Abusive alcoholic parents, disconnected utilities, and overcrowded homes can all affect whether a student stays in school and is able to learn the material. Often, there is a need for children to find work outside the home as soon as they reach a certain age. In other cases, such as my own, the need to escape a bad situation at home leads to teenage marriage, childbirth, and eventually the responsibilities of being a single parent. Students will make better choices if given mentorship and encouragement by caring adults of any race. Growing up in impoverished circumstances can be devastating to the self-esteem of the brightest students who suffer the taunts of their peers.

Problems of Lower-Class Americans

One adult who genuinely cares about a child can make a dramatic difference in life chances. Some of us can remember the first person who ever told us that we were smart and that we were valuable and capable of attaining success. Words of encouragement cost us nothing, yet when they are sincerely offered, they are priceless. Words can change despair into hope and defeat into victory. *Proverbs* 18:21 states, "death and life are in the power of the tongue." An aptly spoken word from an authority figure can change lives forever.

Patsy Partin, a veteran school teacher from Nashville, Tennessee, has found that "low-achieving students often come from a culture of unstable families with poverty, drugs, unwed mothers, and the absence of the father in the home. These non-virtuous characteristics are unacceptable in *any* culture. Such internal, cultural factors work against student achievement." She has mentored many children from such backgrounds, who have gone on to achieve unexpected success because she held them to high standards and failed to stereotype them or reinforce the messages they received from home about their lack of worth.

Unfortunately, the needs and concerns of disadvantaged minorities often seem insurmountable. But as a person who has escaped the worst of lower-class life and emerged on the other side, I am optimistic that collectively we can turn things around. It may take many, many Patsy Partins of all races. But it can be done and it must be done.

Blacks Must Reclaim Their Race

Earl G. Graves, Jr.

Earl G. Graves, Jr., is the founder and publisher of Black Enterprise *magazine and a leading authority on black business development. In 1972 he was named one of the ten most outstanding minority businessmen in the country by President Richard Nixon.*

Both blacks and whites have contributed to the degradation of the American black population, says this author. Such degradation includes diminished academic expectations of black youth, which contributes to worse standards of living as adults; a celebration of criminal behaviors; and "egregious slurs" of language. But the author believes things can be turned around, that African-Americans can reclaim their race. In doing so, blacks will celebrate the victories of their ancestors and allow their children to find success.

There is a plaque in my office that contains a quote by the great John B. Russwurm, editor of *Freedom's Journal*, the first African American-owned and operated newspaper published in the United States. In the first issue, published in 1827, Russwurm wrote: "Too long others have spoken for us. We wish to plead our own cause." Ever since, we as African Americans have endeavored to "plead our own cause"—to define our own identities, our own aspirations, our own paths to economic success and independence.

I, too, felt the calling to "plead our cause" when I founded *Black Enterprise* magazine in August of 1970. In the beginning, I felt that the time had come for a magazine for African

Earl G. Graves, Jr., "We Must Take Back Our Race," *Black Enterprise*, vol. 37, June 2007, pp. 16–18. © 2007 Earl G. Graves Publishing Co., Inc. Republished with permission of Earl G. Graves Publishing Co., Inc., conveyed through Copyright Clearance Center, Inc.

Americans serious about the business of making money that would act as a catalyst for wealth building, entrepreneurship, and financial independence. But with the publishing of our first Top 100 list of the nation's largest black-owned businesses, in our June 1973 issue, we expanded our mission to include an even greater calling: to celebrate our excellence. [This issue of our] magazine, our landmark 35th anniversary issue of the *BE* 100s, continues to champion this calling as we recognize the best and brightest of American industry. . . .

The Time Has Come

Here at *BE*, the celebration of a tradition of excellence among African Americans is part of our culture, our corporate DNA. Sadly, the same cannot be said of our broader culture today. We must dedicate ourselves to reclaiming our excellence. The time has come to take back our race.

Let's be real. The language [radio and television host] Don Imus used to denigrate the outstanding young women of the Rutgers University Scarlet Knights basketball team saturates our own culture. It's in the hip-hop music we produce and consume, the TV shows and movies that we participate in creating, and the so-called "comedy" and "reality shows" that modern-day Amoses and Andys specialize in. [*Amos 'n' Andy* was a radio show in the 1920s and 1930s, in which two white actors played the black characters of the title.] The only difference is that no one has to put on the blackface anymore—we come with our own.

After so many battles won, we have chosen to lower the standards of decency in our own communities, particularly over the past 15 years. One of the consequences of this constant barrage of obscenity and self-hatred has been the utter corruption of how we speak to one another and about one another. And no, I'm not making any excuses for Imus. He's old enough and smart enough to be held accountable for what he says. I'm saying that it's long past time we held accountable all those—regardless of their race or ethnicity—who trade in the degradation of our people. Yes, the time has come to take back our race.

Consider what this degradation has already cost us.

Culture of Low Expectations

How many young African Americans have already given up—surrendered to the apathy and diminished expectations that have engulfed our culture? How many of our children risk ridicule, ostracization, and even violence from their peers for daring to excel academically and to aspire to a life beyond "the street?" The price we are paying for all this is incalculable in many ways, but consider just a few figures: After narrowing the gap in high school dropout rates between blacks and whites during the '70s and '80s, blacks have gained little ground since 1990. The disparity is even more egregious in our urban public schools—in New York City, less than 50% of black students complete high school in four years, compared to more than 70% of white students. Not surprisingly, this culture of low expectations is a particularly damaging contributor to the crisis of young black males. According to the nonprofit Justice Policy Institute, in 1980 black men enrolled in higher education outnumbered those incarcerated by a quarter million. Two decades later, black men behind bars exceeded those on campus by 188,000. That this would negatively impact the stability of black families and communities is obvious. Nearly 43% of black families were headed by single women in 2002, compared to just 13% of white families, according to the U.S. Census Bureau.

How can our young people excel if they are mired in a culture that expects the worst of them; a culture that celebrates criminality; a culture in which the most egregious slurs have replaced terms of love and respect; a culture that entraps them in the depths of society's margins just as surely as any Jim Crow law [laws that encouraged discrimination against blacks, especially after the Civil War through the mid-twentieth century] ever devised? How can we as a people thrive in a culture that denigrates excellence, education, and achievement while glorifying ignorance and mediocrity as authentically black?

We Must Act Now

The answer is, we can't. We must do something about it. We must take back our race. But where we suffer the greatest need for leadership is within our own community. Those of us in positions of power and influence ... must step up. African Americans across the country see our success in business, in politics, in education, in community building. Once again, Black America looks to us for leadership.

How will we answer? I suggest you start by listening to the voices of those who came before us. They fought the hard battles. They stood against the very worst of America's legacy of racism so that we could be here to build our multibillion-dollar companies, to rise to the upper echelons of corporate America and Wall Street, to enable our children to live and dream and achieve. And yet the spirits of our predecessors are troubled and dismayed that we've lost touch with the core values that won us the opportunities so many have chosen to squander.

And so, we must take back our race. If not, where will the next generation of excellence come from? Who will lead the *BE* 100s for the next 35 years? When our children and their children consider us in the bright light of history, what will they think of their inheritance?

I remain committed to upholding our legacy of exellence. I intend to do everything in my power to fulfill my responsibility to take back our race from the diminished expectations and backward mind-set that have taken root in our community. The future of our people, and perhaps our very survival, is on the line.

For Further Discussion

1. Nowhere else are the many identities of Malcolm X more apparent than in his *Autobiography*, which is largely subdivided by chapters named after these identities ("Mascot," "Homeboy," "Detroit Red," "Satan," etc.). As a leader, Malcolm was identified as everything from militant leader to racial justice hero to racist. From your reading of the *Autobiography* and the articles in Chapter 1, how would you summarize the identity of Malcolm X? Do you believe the perception of him has changed since his death? Why or why not?

2. In Chapter 2, the article by David Polizzi speaks of the complex, psychological effects of racism, as seen in feelings of "black antiblackness in an antiblack world." Similarly, George Yancy states, "within the framework of the white imaginary, to be Black and to be human are contradictory terms." In relation to Malcolm X, what do you think each of these writers meant? Do you think such thoughts impact the identity of African-Americans today? Why or why not?

3. In his 1963 *I Have a Dream* speech, Martin Luther King, Jr., said, "I have a dream that one day on the red hills of Georgia the sons of former slaves and the sons of former slave owners will be able to sit down together at the table of brotherhood." In contrast, Malcolm X (before his 1964 trip to Mecca) thought that white/black brotherhood was impossible; even after his trip, he remained doubtful that white/black brotherhood in America was possible. Shortly before his death in 1965, Malcolm predicted: "More and worse riots will erupt. The black man has seen the white man's underbelly of guilty fear." Do you believe King's

hopes have come true, or do you agree with Malcolm X's predictions? Use historical examples and the articles in Chapter 3 as evidence for your answer.

4. In the above Malcolm X quotation, what do you think is meant by "the white man's underbelly of guilty fear"? Do you think this guilty fear has been a driving force of racial tension in the United States? Why or why not? Do you believe such guilty fear exists today?

5. In Chapter 3, Shibley Telhami and Marilyn Elias both write about the increased discrimination against Muslim Americans since the terrorist attacks on the United States on September 11, 2001. But whereas Elias believes the increased discrimination has been severe enough to cause mental health problems, Telhami claims that it is not as bad as some people think. What do you believe? Have you witnessed discrimination against Muslims Americans, in person or on television or radio? What do you believe might improve the situation?

6. In Chapter 3, Earl G. Graves, Jr., insists that the African-American community must work together to overthrow negative cultural images and reclaim their race. "How can our young people excel," he asks, "if they are mired in a culture that expects the worst of them; a culture that celebrates criminality; a culture in which the most egregious slurs have replaced terms of love and respect; a culture that entraps them in the depths of society's margins just as surely as any Jim Crow law ever devised? How can we as a people thrive in a culture that denigrates excellence, education, and achievement while glorifying ignorance and mediocrity as authentically black?" Do you agree with Graves? Do you believe that the current hip-hop culture severely damages African-American culture? Why or why not?

For Further Reading

George Breitman, *Malcolm X Speaks: Selected Speeches and Statements*. New York: Grove Weidenfeld, 1990.

Ralph Ellison, *Invisible Man*. New York: Random House, 1952.

Alex Haley, *A Different Kind of Christmas*. New York: Gramercy Books, 2000.

Alex Haley, *Roots: The Saga of an American Family*. Garden City, New York: Doubleday, 1976.

Alex Haley and David Stevens, *Alex Haley's Queen: The Story of an American Family*. New York: William Morrow, 1993.

Alex Haley and David Stevens, *Mama Flora's Family: A Novel*. New York: Scribner, 1998.

Malcolm X, *By Any Means Necessary*. 2nd ed. New York: Pathfinder, 1992.

Bruce Perry, *Malcolm X: The Last Speeches*. New York: Pathfinder, 1989.

Richard A. Wright, *Black Boy: A Record of Childhood and Youth*. New York: Harper & Brothers, 1945.

Richard A. Wright, *Native Son*. New York: Harper & Brothers, 1940.

Bibliography

Books

James Baldwin *One Day When I Was Lost: A Scenario Based on Alex Haley's The Autobiography of Malcolm X*. New York: Vintage International, 2007.

David Gallen *Malcolm X: As They Knew Him*. New York: Carroll & Graf, 1992.

Kathlyn Gay *Cultural Diversity: Conflicts and Challenges: The Ultimate Teen Guide*. Lanham, MD: Scarecrow Press, 2003.

Peter Louis Goldman *The Death and Life of Malcolm X*. 2nd ed. Urbana, IL: University of Illinois Press, 1979.

Dilara Hafiz *The American Muslim Teenager's Handbook*. Phoenix: Acacia Publishing, 2007.

Alex Haley *Alex Haley: The Man Who Traced America's Roots*. Pleasantville, NY: Reader's Digest Association, 2007.

Andrew Helfer and Randy DuBurke *Malcolm X: A Graphic Biography*. 1st ed. New York: Hill and Wang, 2006.

David Howard-Pitney *Martin Luther King, Jr., Malcolm X, and the Civil Rights Struggle of the 1950s and 1960s: A Brief History with Documents*. New York: Bedford/St. Martin's, 2004.

Diane McWhorter — *A Dream of Freedom: The Civil Rights Movement from 1954 to 1968.* New York: Scholastic, 2004.

Toni Morrison — *Remember: The Journey to School Integration.* Boston: Houghton Mifflin, 2004.

Walter Dean Myers — *Now Is Your Time!: The African-American Struggle for Freedom.* New York: HarperCollins, 1991.

Haroon Siddiqui — *Being Muslim: A Groundwork Guide.* Toronto: Groundwood Books, 2006.

Steven Tsoukalas — *The Nation of Islam: Understanding the "Black Muslims".* Phillipsburg, New Jersey: P&R, 2001.

Periodicals

Tim Appelo — "Alex Haley's Final Passage." *Entertainment Weekly*, February 21, 1992.

Eric Arnesen — "Power Never Takes a Step Back." *Footsteps* 8, no. 2 (March–April 2006): 30–32.

Steven Barboza and Chester Higgins, Jr. — "Facing Mecca." *Essence*, November 1995.

Marty Bell — "Alex Haley: Tale of a Talker." *New York* 10, no. 9 (February 28, 1997): 50–51.

Diana L. Eck   "Muslim in America." *Christian Century* 118, no. 18 (June 6, 2001): 20–26.

The Economist   "Race, Justice and Jena: Black Leadership in America." *The Economist*, September 29, 2007.

Ferruccio   "The Transgression of a Laborer:
Gambino   Malcolm X in the Wilderness of America." *Radical History Review*, no. 55 (Winter 1993): 7.

Thomas K. Grose   "Toward Equality for All." *U.S. News & World Report*, September 22, 2003: 70–73.

James Loomis   "Death of Malcolm X." *New York Times*, February 27, 1965.

Adam Parker   "Civil Rights Group Seeks Young Hearts and Minds." *Charleston Post and Courier*, May 20, 2007.

Gordon Parks   "The White Devil's Day Is Almost Over." *Life*, May 31, 1963.

Bruce Perry   "Malcolm X and the Politics of Masculinity." *Psychohistory Review* 13 (Winter 1985): 18–25.

Jim Sleeper   "Toward an End of Blackness: An Argument for the Surrender of Race Consciousness." *Harper's*, May 1997.

Lynn Speakman   "Who Killed Malcolm X?" *The Valley Advocate*, November 26, 1992.

Daniel Wood "America's Black Muslims Close a Rift." *Christian Science Monitor*, February 14, 2002.

Index

CPSIA information can be obtained
at www.ICGtesting.com
Printed in the USA
FSOW02n1045160917
38746FS